Beautiful Cakes

PEGGY PORSCHEN

Beautiful Cakes

PEGGY PORSCHEN

PHOTOGRAPHY BY GEORGIA GLYNN SMITH

BARNES & NOBLE
NEW YORK

For Bryn with love

Photographs © 2007 Georgia Glynn Smith
Edited text, design & layout © 2007 Quadrille Publishing Ltd

Editorial Director: Jane O'Shea
Creative Director: Helen Lewis
Editor and Project Manager: Lewis Esson
Art Director: Chalkley Calderwood
Photography: Georgia Glynn Smith
Production: Ruth Deary

ISBN-13: 978-0-7607-9179-0
ISBN-10: 0-7607-9179-1

Library of Congress Cataloging-in-Publication Data is available.

Printed and bound in China.

10 9 8 7 6 5 4 3 2 1

Contents

Cookies

Luscious Lips

These cookie kisses make an ideal Valentine's Day gift. The bolder the colors, the better—here I used vibrant reds and pinks, with a sprinkle of edible glitter.

FOR ABOUT 20 COOKIES

about 14 oz. royal icing (see page 136)

pink and red food colors

10 to 12 gingerbread cookies in the shape of
   lips, about 2½x4 in., made
   using 1 recipe quantity of gingerbread
   cookie dough (see page 119)

magenta edible glitter

red edible glitter

TOOLS

2 SMALL BOWLS

SMALL ICING SPATULA

PAPER DECORATING BAGS (SEE PAGE 137)

PAIR OF SCISSORS

PLASTIC WRAP OR DAMP CLOTH

SOFT BRUSH

1 Divide the royal icing equally between 2 bowls. Mix one amount of icing with pink food color, the other with red. Add a little water until the icing reaches soft-peak consistency (see page 137). Fill one decorating bag with each color.

2 Snip a small tip off each decorating bag and pipe around the sides of the lips in a steady, smooth line (see 1 on page 138). Outline red lips with the red icing and pink lips with the pink icing. Cover the decorating bags with plastic wrap or a damp cloth to prevent the icing drying.

3 Dilute the remaining pink and red icings with a few drops of water to make each a runny consistency (see page 137). Fill one decorating bag of each color and flood the middles of the cookies (see 2), being careful not to overflow at the sides. For those with glitter, sprinkle a light dusting in the appropriate color over the wet icing; let dry.

4 Once the cookies are dry, brush the excess glitter off them where required and then pipe the detail on each cookie (see 3), using the reserved soft-peak icing. To enhance the lip shape, pipe the detail for the red lips with pink icing and the detail for the pink lips with red icing; let dry.

Butterflies Away

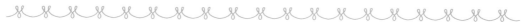

I originally developed the idea for this table centerpiece with Vanessa Gore for a feature in *You & Your Wedding* magazine. You can find beautiful antique-style birdcages at markets or interior-decorating or antique stores, but they are also available for rent. For a butterfly-themed wedding reception, combine these centerpieces with my Butterfly Miniature Wedding Cakes on pages 44–5.

FOR 15 COOKIES

15 cookies in 3 different shapes and sizes of butterfly, made using 1 recipe quantity of sugar cookie dough (see page 118)

about 1¼ lb. royal icing (see page 136)

TOOLS

SMALL ROUND CUTTER

SMALL BOWL

SMALL ICING SPATULA

PAPER DECORATING BAGS (SEE PAGE 137)

PAIR OF SCISSORS

PLASTIC WRAP OR DAMP CLOTH

1 YD. WHITE RIBBON

1 As soon as the cookies come out of the oven, cut a little hole at the top of one wing on each, using the small round cutter; leave them to cool on a wire rack.

2 Once the cookies are cool, start by mixing the icing with a little water until it reaches soft-peak consistency (see page 137). Put some of the icing into a decorating bag.

3 Snip a small tip off the bag and pipe the outlines of the wings (see page 138). Keep the bag with the leftover icing covered with plastic wrap or a damp cloth to prevent the icing drying out.

4 Dilute the remaining icing with a few drops of water to a runny consistency (see page 137). Put into a fresh decorating bag. Again, snip the tip off the bag and fill the middle of the wings with the runny icing, being careful not to overflow the sides; let dry.

5 Once the cookies are dry, pipe the body and the detail, such as swirls and small dots, onto the wings, using the soft-peak icing; let dry.

6 Once the cookies are completely dry (ideally leave overnight), push a piece of ribbon through each hole and carefully hang them inside and outside the birdcage.

Bride and Groom Cookies

Use these as wedding favors or as a token to accompany your gift.
To add a personal touch, match the designs to the real wedding gowns.

FOR 3 BRIDE AND 3 GROOM COOKIES

about 1¼ lb. royal icing (see page 136)

black food color

3 cookies made in the shape of prom dresses
(about 5x4 in.) and 3 in the
shape of tuxedos (about 3x4½ in.)
made using 1 recipe quantity
of sugar cookie dough (see page 118)

TOOLS

2 SMALL BOWLS

SMALL ICING SPATULA

PAPER DECORATING BAGS (SEE PAGE 137)

PAIR OF SCISSORS

PLASTIC WRAP OR DAMP CLOTH

➤1 Divide the icing between two bowls, about 9 ounces in one and 12 ounces in the other. Mix the 9 ounces with black food color. Add a little water to both bowls until the icings reach soft-peak consistency (see page 137). Fill one decorating bag with each color.

➤2 Snip a small tip off the bag with black icing and pipe the outline of each tuxedo in a steady smooth line (see 1 on page 138). Do the same with the white icing on the gown cookies. Cover the bags with plastic wrap or a damp cloth to prevent the icing drying out.

➤3 Dilute the remaining white and black icing with a few drops of water to a runny consistency (see page 137). Fill one decorating bag with each color and flood the middles of the cookies in the appropriate colors, being careful not to overflow the sides. Flood the tuxedo middles with white first (see 2), let dry, and then flood the black part (see 3).

➤4 Once dry, pipe the detail on each cookie, using the soft-peak icing (see 4); let dry.

Heart-Shaped Place Cards

This clever idea turns a simple heart cookie into a stunning decorative feature at the dinner table of a wedding or engagement party. You can use other cookie shapes as well, as long as they provide enough space for writing names on the top. If you find using the ribbon too fiddly, wrap each heart in a cellophane bag and place it on top of each dinner plate. This way your guests can take the cookie home as a personalized keepsake.

FOR 10 COOKIES

10 cookies made in heart shapes (about
   2½ in.) using ½ recipe quantity
   of sugar cookie dough (see page 118)
12 oz. royal icing (see page 136)
dusky-pink and dark-brown food colors

TOOLS

SMALL ROUND CUTTER
SMALL BOWL
SMALL ICING SPATULA
PAPER DECORATING BAGS (SEE PAGE 137)
PAIR OF SCISSORS
PLASTIC WRAP OR DAMP CLOTH
1½ YD. PASTEL-PINK RIBBON, ⅜ IN. WIDE

1 As soon as the heart cookies come out of the oven, cut a little hole at the top of each, using the small round cutter. Be careful as the tray will be hot; leave them to cool.

2 Once the cookies are cool, start with the brown outline. In a bowl, mix about 10 ounces icing with a small amount of brown color. Add a little water until it reaches soft-peak consistency (see page 137). Put some of the icing into a decorating bag. Snip a small tip off the decorating bag and pipe around the outlines of the hearts (see page 138).

3 If you have any icing left over in the bag, squeeze it back into the bowl with the remaining brown icing and dilute it with a few drops of water to a runny consistency (see page 137). Put this into a fresh decorating bag. Again, snip the tip off and fill the middles of each cookie with the runny icing, being careful not to overflow the sides; let dry.

4 Once dry, mix the remaining royal icing with dusky-pink food color and a little water to soft-peak consistency. Put it into a decorating bag, snip off a small tip, and pipe a squiggly outline around the sides of the hearts. Pipe names or initials in the middle; let dry.

5 Once completely dry (ideally leave overnight), push a piece of ribbon through the hole and tie into a knot or a bow. Attach to a champagne glass or a napkin as a place card.

Rosebud Cookies

To complement the rosebud design, I have scented the icing with rosewater. Wrapped in a pretty gift box or cellophane bags, these gorgeous little cookies make an exquisite gift or wedding favor.

FOR ABOUT 12 COOKIES

about 1 lb. royal icing (see page 136)

red, pink, and green food colors

small amount of rosewater

12 cookies in the shape of rosebuds, made from 1 recipe quantity of vanilla sugar cookie dough (see page 118)

TOOLS

SEVERAL SMALL BOWLS

SMALL ICING SPATULA

FEW PAPER DECORATING BAGS (SEE PAGE 137)

PAIR OF SCISSORS

PLASTIC WRAP OR DAMP CLOTH

1 Place about 10 ounces royal icing in a bowl and color it with red food color. Add a few drops of rosewater until the icing reaches soft-peak consistency (see page 137). Put a small amount in a decorating bag.

2 Snip a small tip off the decorating bag and pipe the outlines for the flowering top of the buds on the cookies, leaving enough space for the green leaves at the bottom of the cookies. Pipe all the red outlines first.

3 If you have any red icing left over in the bag, squeeze it back into the bowl with the remaining red icing and dilute it with a few drops of rosewater to a runny consistency (see page 137). Put this in a fresh decorating bag. Again, snip a tip off the decorating bag and fill the red-outline middles of the bud heads with the runny icing, being careful not to overflow the sides; let dry before piping on the green stems and leaves.

4 Once the red icing is completely dry, color about $3\frac{1}{2}$ ounces of icing green. Put a small amount in a decorating bag and pipe the outline of the stems first, then, as in step 3, make some runny green icing and flood the middles with that and fill the middles of the stems; let dry. Reserve a small amount of soft-peak green icing to trace the outline of the stems and leaves later.

5 Mix the remaining 2 ounces icing with pink food color and trace the individual petals of the rosebuds; let dry.

6 Once dry, trace the outline of the stems using the reserved green icing; let dry.

Wedding Cake Cookies

This idea gives you the option of coordinating the design of your
wedding favor with your wedding cake, making a lovely memento for your guests
to take home or to send to those who were unable to attend—
those who live far away, for example.

FOR 6 COOKIES

1¼ lb. royal icing (see page 136)

baby-blue food color

6 cookies in the shape of wedding cakes
   (about 4x5 in.), made using
   1 recipe quantity of sugar cookie dough,
   see page 118)

TOOLS

SMALL BOWL

SMALL ICING SPATULA

PAPER DECORATING BAGS (SEE PAGE 137)

PAIR OF SCISSORS

PLASTIC WRAP OR DAMP CLOTH

1 In a small bowl, mix about 1 pound royal icing with a little water to soft-peak consistency (see page 137). Put some of the icing into a decorating bag.

2 Snip a small tip off the decorating bag and pipe the outline of the cake shape for each cookie in a steady, smooth line (see page 138). Cover the piping bag with the leftover icing with plastic wrap or a damp cloth to prevent it drying out.

3 Dilute the remaining icing with a few drops of water to a runny consistency (see page 137). Put it in a decorating bag and flood the middles of the cookies, being careful not to overflow the sides; let dry.

4 Once dry, mix the remaining 5 ounces icing with a little blue food color and a small amount of water to make a soft-peak consistency (see page 137). Pipe the outline of the bow detail on each cookie. Cover the decorating bag with any leftover icing with plastic wrap or a damp cloth to prevent it drying out.

5 Dilute the remaining blue icing with a small amount of water to a runny consistency (see page 137), put it in a decorating bag, and use to flood the middle of the bow; let dry.

6 With the reserved soft-peak white icing, pipe the outline for the individual cake tiers and a dotted border at the bottom. With the reserved soft-peak blue icing, pipe the detail of the bow; let dry.

Risqué Lingerie

Make little goodie bags filled with these lingerie cookies
for friends at your shower. If you are already married, make them for your
husband to give him a taste of what is in store for later.

FOR ABOUT 4 **ONE-PIECE LINGERIE**
COOKIES AND 4 **TWO-PIECE COOKIES**

1¼ lb. royal icing (see page 136)

pink and red food colors

4 cookies in the shape of a one-piece swim
    suit (about 2½x4 in.) and
    4 cookies each in the shape of bras and
    panties (about 3-in. square),
    made using 1 recipe quantity of sugar or
    gingerbread cookie dough (see pages 118–19)

TOOLS

3 SMALL BOWLS

SMALL ICING SPATULA

PAPER DECORATING BAGS (SEE PAGE 137)

PAIR OF SCISSORS

PLASTIC WRAP OR DAMP CLOTH

➤1 Divide the royal icing equally between 3 small bowls. Color one with pink and one
with red food color, and keep the third one white. Add a small amount of water to each
until the icing reaches soft-peak consistency (see page 137). Put a small amount of each
color into a decorating bag and keep the remaining icing covered with plastic wrap or a
damp cloth to prevent it drying out.

➤2 Snip a small tip off each bag and pipe the outlines for the bras, the panties and
the camisoles for each cookie (see 1). Keep the decorating bags covered with plastic wrap
to prevent the icing from drying out.

➤3 Dilute the icing remaining in the bowls with a small amount of water to a runny
consistency (see page 137) and put into 3 fresh decorating bags. Flood the centers of each
cookie with the same color as the outline, then use a different color to pipe little dots on
the still-wet base (see 2). This way the dots will sink in and form a smooth surface with
the main icing; let dry.

➤4 Once everything is dry,
pipe the details, such as the
frills, straps, and little bows,
using the reserved soft-peak
icing (see 3); let dry.

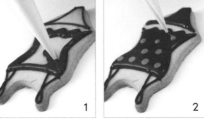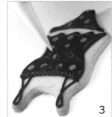

Celestial Lovers

The twinkling stars and golden moon have inspired lovers since the beginning of time. There is more than a hint of night-sky magic about these little cookies.

FOR 5 CRESCENT MOONS AND 15 STAR COOKIES

about 14 oz. royal icing (see page 136)

black food color

5 cookies in the shape of crescent moons (about 2x4 in.) and 15 in the shape of small stars (about 1½ in.), made using 1 recipe quantity of sugar cookie dough (see page 118)

silver glitter sparkle

TOOLS

SMALL BOWL

SMALL ICING SPATULA

PAPER DECORATING BAGS (SEE PAGE 137)

PAIR OF SCISSORS

SOFT BRUSH FOR DUSTING

PLASTIC WRAP OR DAMP CLOTH

▸**1** Place the royal icing in a bowl and mix it with a small amount of black food color to a light gray shade. Add a little water until the icing reaches soft-peak consistency (see page 137). Put some of the icing into a decorating bag. Keep the remaining icing covered with plastic wrap or a damp cloth to prevent it drying out.

▸**2** Snip a small tip off the decorating bag and pipe the outlines of the moon and the stars in a steady, smooth line (see page 138).

▸**3** Dilute the remaining icing with a few drops of water to a runny consistency (see page 137). Fill a fresh decorating bag with this.

▸**4** Again snip off the tip and fill the middle of each cookie with the runny icing, being careful not to overflow the sides.

▸**5** While the icing is still wet, drizzle a small amount of glitter over the cookies and then let dry.

▸**6** Once the icing is dry, carefully use the soft brush to dust the excess glitter off the cookies.

Carnival in Venice

I made these as wedding favors for my mother-in-law to be, Georgina Harvey, and her new husband, Rog, and dedicate this design to them. Their wedding theme was Venetian, and the white mask is an almost exact copy of the one the bride wore. All their guests got masks, too, so I added sticks to the white ones for the ladies, and ribbons to the men's golden masks to tie them around their heads.

FOR 10 COOKIES

1 recipe quantity of gingerbread cookie dough
  (see page 119)

1¼ lb. royal icing (see page 136)

ivory food color

gold edible glitter

gold luster

small amount of clear alcohol

small amount of gum paste

small amount of confectioners' sugar

TOOLS

SMALL NONSTICK PLASTIC BOARD

SMALL ROLLING PIN

5 COOKIE STICKS

MASK AND EYE CUTTERS

SMALL KITCHEN KNIFE

BAKING TRAY

WIRE RACK

2 SMALL BOWLS

SMALL ICING SPATULA

PLASTIC WRAP OR DAMP CLOTH

PAPER DECORATING BAGS (SEE PAGE 137)

PAIR OF SCISSORS

SOFT BRUSH FOR DUSTING

FINE ARTIST'S BRUSH

6 YD. THIN GOLD RIBBON

2 FLOWER CUTTERS (1 LARGE, 1 SMALL)

COLOR MIXING SPATULA

3 YD. IVORY AND GOLD RIBBON

1 On a nonstick plastic board, roll out half the cookie dough until about ½ inch thick. Place about one-third of a cookie stick underneath the dough and keep rolling the dough over the stick until the dough is just about ¹⁄₁₆ inch thicker than the stick.

2 Place the mask cutter over the top, with the cookie stick to one side. Push down and cut around the cutter with a small knife where necessary. Use the separate eye-shaped cutter to cut out eye holes; carefully transfer to a baking tray. Repeat until you have 5 masks on sticks. Repeat the rolling and cutting without sticks to make 5 more masks.

3 Bake as described on page 119 and leave to cool on a wire rack.

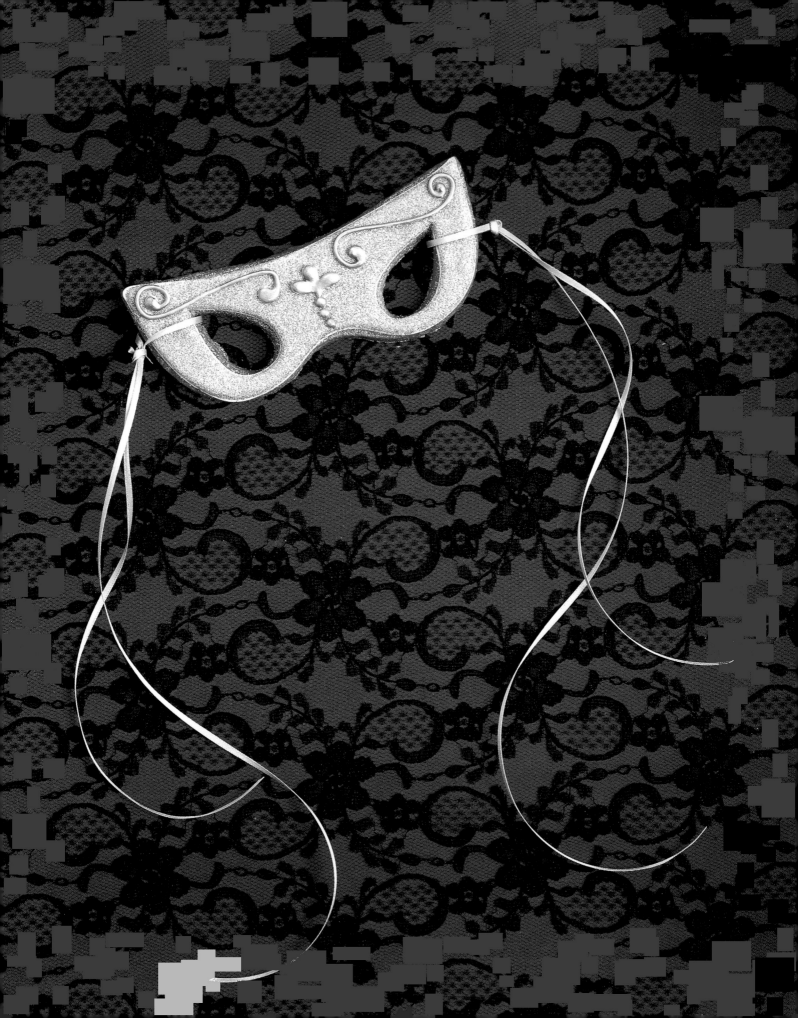

4 Place 10 ounces royal icing in a small bowl. Mix in enough ivory food color to produce a strong ivory color Add a few drops of water and mix to a soft-peak consistency (see page 137). Put some of the icing into a decorating bag. Keep the remaining icing covered.

5 Snip a small tip off the bag and pipe the outline of the gold masks in a smooth steady line (see page 138). Cover the bag with plastic wrap or a damp cloth to prevent it drying out.

6 Add a little more water to the remaining icing to produce a runny consistency (see page 137). Put it into a fresh decorating bag and use to flood the cookie middles.

7 While the icing is still wet, sprinkle a light dusting of gold glitter over the top and then let dry completely. Once the icing on the cookies is dry, brush off the excess glitter.

8 Use the bag of soft-peak ivory icing to pipe a swirl design around the eyes; let dry.

9 Once the swirls are dry, mix a small amount of gold luster with a drop of alcohol to a thick paste. Use a fine artist's brush to paint the swirls with the gold; let dry overnight.

10 Once dry, tie a piece of gold ribbon through the holes for the eyes on each side.

TO MAKE THE IVORY MASKS

11 Place the remaining icing in another small bowl and color to a pale ivory. Add a few drops of water and mix to a soft-peak consistency. Put some into a decorating bag. Keep the remaining icing covered.

12 Repeat steps 5 and 6, using the pale ivory icing.

13 Make the sugar flowers. Roll the gum paste out on the plastic board dusted with confectioners' sugar until very thin. Cut out a selection of little sugar flowers.

14 Place each flower into a well of the color-mixing palette to let them dry: This way they will dry in a rounded/curved shape.

15 Once the icing is dry, stick the little flowers on top using a small dab of icing.

16 Using a decorating bag filled with ivory soft-peak royal icing, pipe the swirls and dots around the eyes and the flower middles; let dry overnight.

17 Finish the cookies by tying a bow of ribbon around the top of each cookie stick.

Mini Heart Favors

For obvious reasons, iced heart-shaped cookies are among the most popular choices for wedding favors. What makes this particular version so pretty is wrapping the three different shades of pink together in a bag. This idea works for any color scheme. Instead of using them as favors, you can serve them individually as petits fours, arranged on a cake stand or at the side of a coffeecup.

FOR 24 COOKIES

about 10 oz. royal icing (see page 136)
pink food color
24 cookies in small heart shapes (about
1½ in.), made using ½ recipe quantity
    of sugar cookie dough (see page 118)

TOOLS

SMALL BOWL
SMALL ICING SPATULA
PAPER DECORATING BAGS (SEE PAGE 137)
PAIR OF SCISSORS
PLASTIC WRAP OR DAMP CLOTH
8 CELLOPHANE BAGS (OPTIONAL)
ABOUT 5 YD. PINK SATIN RIBBON (OPTIONAL)

1 Start with the lightest shade of pink. In a bowl, mix one-third of the royal icing with a tiny drop of pink food color to make a pastel-pink shade. Add a little water until the icing is soft-peak consistency (see page 137). Put some of the icing into a decorating bag; keep the bowl covered.

2 Snip a small tip off the decorating bag and pipe the outline of the heart in a steady, smooth line (see page 138). Outline 8 of the hearts with the pastel-pink icing.

3 If you have any icing left over in the bag, squeeze it back into the bowl with the remaining pastel-pink icing and dilute it with a few drops of water to a runny consistency (see page 137). Fill a fresh decorating bag with this.

4 Again snip off the tip and fill the middle of the hearts with the runny icing, being careful not to let it overflow the sides.

5 Repeat steps 1 to 4, using 2 darker shades of pink icing, so you have 8 cookies in each shade.

6 If you like, you can pack 1 of each shade of cookie in a cellophane bag and tie decoratively with ribbon.

Tea for Two

These funky retro-inspired teapots and teacups make the perfect
addition to a vintage-style bridal shower.

FOR 4 TEAPOT AND 4 TEACUP COOKIES

about 1¼ lb. royal icing (see page 136)

pink, blue, and green food colors

4 cookies in the shape of teapots (about
    3x4 in.) and 4 in the shape of

teacups (about 3x3½ in.),

made using 1 recipe quantity of sugar
    cookie dough (see page 118)

TOOLS

3 SMALL BOWLS

SMALL ICING SPATULA

PAPER DECORATING BAGS (SEE PAGE 137)

PAIR OF SCISSORS

PLASTIC WRAP OR DAMP CLOTH

1 Divide the royal icing equally between 3 bowls. Mix one amount of icing with pink
and one with blue food color, and keep the other one white. Add a little water to all
3 bowls until they have reached soft-peak consistency (see page 137). Fill one decorating
bag with each color.

2 One at a time, snip a small tip off each decorating bag and pipe the outline of each
cookie in a steady, smooth line (see page 138), decorating one cup and one teapot in each
color. Cover the decorating bags with plastic wrap or a damp cloth to prevent the icing
drying out.

3 Dilute each of the remaining bowls of icing with a few drops of water to a runny
consistency (see page 137). Fill one decorating bag with each color and flood the middles
of the appropriately colored cookies, being careful not to let the icing overflow the sides.

4 Once they are dry, pipe the outlines, including the lids and handles, using a contrast-
ing color (white on pink or blue on white), using the soft-peak icing.

5 Using the soft-peak icing, pipe different designs on each cookie, such as polka dots,
stripes, hearts, and little rosebuds. For the little leaves of the rosebuds, mix some leftover white icing with green food color, snip the tip of the decorating bag in a V shape
and pipe the leaves; let dry.

Heart-Shaped Sugar Cubes

Although this doesn't involve baking, I couldn't resist adding this simple but very sweet idea to my romantic portfolio. You can use any shape you like.

FOR ABOUT 12 SUGAR CUBES

about 6 tablespoons sugar
pink, blue, and yellow food colors

TOOLS

SMALL BOWLS
WAX PAPER
SMALL HEART-SHAPED COOKIE CUTTER
TEASPOON

1 Divide the sugar equally between 3 small bowls, then add a tiny drop of each food color and a little water to each to make it damp; mix until evenly colored.

2 On a piece of wax paper, push a small amount of sugar firmly into the heart cutter (see 1) and smooth the top with a spoon (see 2). Carefully lift off the cutter and let the sugar heart dry (see 3 and 4).

3 Repeat until all the sugar in each color is used.

Mini Cakes

Je T'aime Mon Amour...

This simple presentation of little alphabet cakes makes a
uniquely personal gift. You can ice any message in this way, or even make it
more intriguing by arranging the letters randomly as a kind of puzzle,
letting the recipient put the message together.

**FOR A MESSAGE LIKE THIS ONE,
OF ABOUT 15 LETTERS**

about 15 fondant fancies made as
    described on pages 133–4, using a
    6-in. square Victoria sponge cake
    (½ recipe quantity, see the guide on
    page 143) and red fondant icing
about ½ lb. royal icing
pink and red food colors

TOOLS

ABOUT 15 ROUND SILVER METALLIC BAKING
    CUPS (THEY DON'T MAKE SQUARE ONES,
    BUT THESE MOLD TO SHAPE)
SMALL BOWL
SMALL ICING SPATULA
PAPER DECORATING BAGS (SEE PAGE 137)
PAIR OF SCISSORS
GIFT BOX, WRAPPING PAPER, AND RIBBON
    (OPTIONAL)

1 Place the fondant fancies into the silver baking cups. Only round baking cups are
usually available, so you need to shape them around the fondant fancies (see page 134).

2 Place about 7 ounces royal icing in a small bowl. Using a small spatula, mix it with
pink food color and a few drops of water until at soft-peak consistency (see page 137). Fill
some of the icing into a decorating bag and keep the remainder in the covered bowl.

3 Snip the tip off a decorating bag and pipe the outlines of the letters on the fondant
fancies.

4 If you have any icing left inside the bag, squeeze it back into the bowl and dilute the
icing with water, this time to a runny consistency (see page 137). Put this in a new
decorating bag and use to flood the letter middles. Be careful not to let the icing
overflow the sides.

5 Mix the remaining icing with red food color and enough water to achieve a slight
runny consistency. Put it in a fresh decorating bag, snip off a small tip, and pipe little
dots into the still-wet pink icing of the letters; let dry.

6 Arrange the cakes to spell out your personal message (or jumble them) in a gift box,
if you like.

Chocolate Bow Candy Cakes

These cakes are ideal for a small wedding, as you can make a tiered
miniature wedding cake per guest instead of one large wedding cake.
And, they travel well and look very pretty in a clear gift box,
they also make stunning wedding favors.

FOR ABOUT 6 MINI TIERED WEDDING CAKES

confectioners' sugar for dusting

about 9 oz. ready-made gum paste colored
   dark brown

edible glue

six 3-in. and six 1½-in. round cakes, made from
   a 12-in. square rich dark chocolate cake
   (see page 124), flavored and soaked to
   choice, then covered with marzipan and
   pastel-blue, green, and yellow rolled fondant
   icing (2 of each type of cake in each color,
   see pages 125–8)

small amount of royal icing (see page 136)

dark-brown and willow-green (Wilton)
   food colors

TOOLS

PLASTIC WRAP OR DAMP CLOTH

SMALL NONSTICK PLASTIC BOARD

SMALL ROLLING PIN

SMALL KITCHEN KNIFE

DESIGN WHEELER

SMALL BRUSH

PAPER TOWELS

BOW CUTTER

FOR THE BLUE CAKES

1 On a plastic board dusted with confectioners' sugar, roll out the gum paste and cut it
into strips ⅜ inch wide, then roll the design wheeler along the edges.

2 To make each bow, cut a strip 4 inches long and turn upside down. Fold both ends over
and glue down in the middle, supporting the loops with paper towels. Cut another strip
about 1¼ inches long, fold it over the seam, and secure it with edible glue; let dry.

3 Cut 4 strips about 6 inches long and lay them down the sides of the cake, fixing them
with edible glue. Cut 4 thin strips to place in between the spaces at the bottom.

4 To finish each bow, cut 2 more pieces of brown gum paste about 1½ inches long and
snip the ends in a V shape. Stick on the top tier with edible glue, then add the bow.

5 On a plastic board dusted with confectioners' sugar, thinly roll out the brown gum paste. Cut out the shapes for the bows using the bow cutter. Assemble the bows as before; let dry.

6 Divide the top tier of the green cake into 3 and the bottom tier into 5 even parts around the edges and mark them with small dots. These are the points where the bows will be attached.

7 Roll out another piece of brown gum paste and cut out strips about ½ inch wide and 1½ to 2½ inches long.

8 Twist each strip with your fingers and attach to the sides of the cake with edible glue.

9 Now stick the brown bows on top of the seams, using a small amount of chocolate-brown royal icing.

10 Mix a small amount of icing with green color to soft-peak consistency (see page 137) and pipe small dots around the bottom of each tier.

FOR THE YELLOW CAKES

11 On a plastic board dusted with confectioners' sugar, thinly roll out the brown gum paste. Cut out a ¼ inch thin strip to go around the base of the bottom tier and a 1 inch wide strip to go around the base of the top tier. Fix them both in place with edible glue.

12 To make the bow, cut out a ⅝-inch wide and 4-inch long strip from the brown gum paste, then fold both ends over to the middle and glue them down, supporting the loops with paper towels. Cut another strip about 1¼ inches long, then fold it over the seam and secure it with edible glue; let dry.

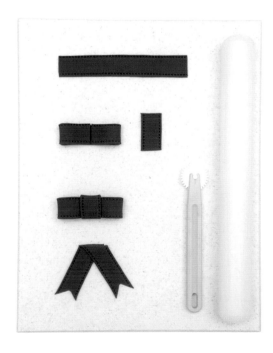

13 To finish the bow, cut 2 more pieces of brown gum paste about 1½ inches long and snip the ends off in a V shape. Place them on the side of the top tier with brown icing or edible glue, then stick the bow on top.

Forget-Me-Not Fancies

These little delights make perfect cakes for a celebration tea or can be served as petits fours. The forget-me-not motif also makes them a great idea for a token to wish someone farewell—say, a bride and groom going on honeymoon.

FOR 16 FONDANT FANCIES

16 fondant fancies (made as described on pages 133–4) using a 6-in. square Victoria sponge cake flavored to your choice and dipped in pastel-lilac fondant icing

about 3½ oz. white gum paste

blue and yellow food colors

confectioners' sugar or cornstarch for dusting

small amount of royal icing (see page 136)

TOOLS

16 METALLIC SILVER BAKING CUPS

NONSTICK BOARD WITH HOLES (CEL BOARD)

SMALL ROLLING PIN

SMALL 5-PETAL FLOWER CUTTER

BONE TOOL

PETAL FLUTING/POINTED END TOOL

STAYFRESH MULTI MAT

PAPER DECORATING BAGS (SEE PAGE 137)

PAIR OF SCISSORS

1 Place the fondant fancies in silver baking cups as described on page 134.

2 Color the gum paste pastel blue by kneading in a small amount of the color.

3 Lightly dust the plastic board with confectioners' sugar and place a small piece of the paste over the medium-size hole, then roll the paste out until very thin. Turn the paste upside down and place your flower cutter over the area of the raised knot and cut out the flower.

4 Carefully lift the flower and curve it around the bone tool to form a cup. Gently push the tip of the pointed tool into the middle of the flower; let dry. Make about 48 the same way.

5 Once the curved flowers are dry, stick a cluster of "forget-me-nots" onto each fondant fancy using small dabs of royal icing.

6 Mix a small amount of royal icing with yellow food color, put it in a decorating bag, snip a small tip off the bag, and pipe little yellow dots in the middle of the flowers.

7 Squeeze the remaining icing out off the bag, add a drop of blue color, and mix to a soft green. Put in a fresh bag, snip a V shape in the tip, and pipe little leaves around the flowers.

Butterfly Miniature Wedding Cakes

The mix of butterflies in different sizes, some on their own and some in pairs, gives each individual cake interest to the eye. To create the look of a "living swarm" of butterflies I have arranged some individual butterflies on the pillars and the tiers of the cake stand. As a symbol of love and union, a large butterfly couple decorates the top tier, which can be used as the cutting cake.

FOR ABOUT 25 MINIATURE CAKES AND 1 6-IN. TOP TIER CAKE

small amount of shortening

about 12 oz. royal icing

25 miniature cakes (2-in. diameter)
cut from a 12-in. square of sponge
cake and one 6-in. round cake,
made using 4½ recipe quantities of Victoria
sponge cake mixture, trimmed, soaked, and
flavored to choice, then covered with
marzipan and a thin layer of white rolled
fondant icing as described on pages 127–31

TOOLS

SHEETS OF CELLOPHANE

SMALL BOWL

SMALL ICING SPATULA

PAPER DECORATING BAGS (SEE PAGE 137)

PAIR OF SCISSORS

PLASTIC WRAP OR DAMP CLOTH

THIN CARDBOARD

WAX PAPER

ABOUT 6½ YD. WHITE SATIN RIBBON, ⅝ IN. WIDE

Make the butterflies at least 2 days in advance. You'll need 2 large butterflies for the top tier and about 20 medium and 20 small ones.

▸**1** Place a sheet of cellophane on top of the butterfly template (see inside back cover) and rub it with a very thin layer of shortening.

▸**2** Mix the royal icing with a little water to soft-peak consistency (see page 137) and put some in a decorating bag. Snip a small tip off the bag and pipe the outline for the wings on the cellophane. Keep the icing in the bowl covered with plastic wrap or a damp cloth to prevent it drying out.

▸**3** Dilute about 9 ounces of the icing with a small amount of water to a runny consistency (see page 137). Fill a decorating bag with it and flood the middles of the butterfly wing outlines. To avoid the icing of both wings running together, flood only one part first and let that set before you flood the other part. Let these butterflies dry completely overnight.

4 Once dry, decorate the wings with piped swirls and dots, using soft-peak royal icing; let dry.

5 Take a piece of thin cardboard (I use the lid of a cake box) and fold it like an accordion (see page 80). Then cut a sheet of wax paper into strips to line the cardboard folds.

6 Once the decorated wings are completely dry, carefully lift them off the cellophane. Pipe the bodies for the butterflies into the folds of the wax paper and stick the butterfly wings together as shown on page 80 . Let them dry for a couple of hours to make sure they stick together securely.

TO DECORATE THE CAKES

7 Cut the ribbon into pieces long enough to cover the sides of the cakes and arrange the pieces around the bottom of each cake, securing them with dabs of royal icing.

8 Pipe small dots along the edge of the ribbon, using soft-peak royal icing (see 1).

9 Once the butterflies are dry, stick them on top of the cakes with dabs of icing (see 2). Arrange a few butterfly pairs and a few single ones on top of the miniature cakes and finish the top tier with a large butterfly couple.

Ribbon Rose Cupcakes

These feature a very pretty type of rose made using a simple
technique. As it looks like a piece of ribbon rolled together to form
a little rosebud, I have called it a "ribbon rose."

FOR 12 CUPCAKES

about 8 oz. rolled fondant icing

red, pink, and green food colors

confectioners' sugar for dusting

12 cupcakes, made using 1½ recipe quantities
Victoria sponge cake (see page 122),
flavored to choice, baked in silver metallic
baking cups, soaked with syrup, and iced
with pink and purple fondant icing (see
pages 133–5)

small amount of royal icing (see page 136)

TOOLS

PLASTIC WRAP

SMALL NONSTICK PLASTIC BOARD

SMALL ROLLING PIN

LEAF CUTTER

SMALL KITCHEN KNIFE

PAPER DECORATING BAG (SEE PAGE 137)

PAIR OF SCISSORS

1 Mix about 3 ounces of the rolled fondant with red color, 3 ounces with pink, and
2 ounces with green. Always keep fondant you are not using covered with plastic wrap to
prevent it drying out.

2 On a plastic board lightly dusted with
confectioners' sugar, roll a piece of pink or red
rolled fondant out to about 1¼ inches wide, 3¼
inches long and about ¹⁄₁₆ inch thick. Trim the
edges and fold the strip over in half lengthways
down its width, pinching it at intervals to get a
pleated effect, as shown. Now roll the folded
strip up from one side to the other and pinch off
the excess at the bottom of the flower shape;
let dry. You'll need 6 pink and 6 red roses.

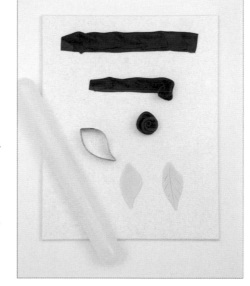

3 For the leaves, roll out a thin piece of green
rolled fondant and cut out 24 leaves using the
leaf cutter. Mark the leaf veins down the middle using a small kitchen knife. Shape the
leaves slightly with your fingers and let dry.

4 Once the roses and leaves are dry, stick them on top of the cupcakes using a dab of
royal icing to fix them in place.

Chocolate Hearts

These little French-style chocolate heart cakes make a delightful alternative to chocolate or chocolate truffles. I used an old-fashioned crimping technique for the border design on the monogram heart, which gives this classic design a touch of "retro revival."

FOR 24 SMALL CAKES

24 small cakes made using 1½ recipe quantities of rich dark chocolate sponge cake (see page 124), baked in miniature heart-shaped baking tins (about 2 in. across)

2 tablespoon strained apricot jam

confectioners' sugar for dusting

about 2¼ lb. dark-brown chocolate-flavored rolled fondant icing

a little edible glue or alcohol

small amount of royal icing (see page 136)

pink food color

about 7 oz. white rolled fondant icing

pink edible luster dust

TOOLS

SMALL KITCHEN KNIFE

SMALL SAUCEPAN

PASTRY BRUSH

ROLLING PIN

1/4-IN. MARZIPAN SPACERS

SERRATED CRIMPING TOOL

SMALL ROLLING PIN WITH A LINED SURFACE

PAPER DECORATING BAGS (SEE PAGE 137)

PAIR OF SCISSORS

SMALL HEART CUTTER

FINE ARTIST'S BRUSH

1 Level the top of the heart cakes by trimming the top crust off each with a kitchen knife. Gently heat the apricot jam and thinly brush it all over the little cakes.

2 On a smooth surface dusted with confectioners' sugar, roll out the chocolate rolled fondant between the marzipan spacers into a piece large enough to cover the top and sides of all the cakes. Lay the rolled fondant over the cakes and carefully push it down the sides. Trim off the excess fondant using a kitchen knife.

FOR THE MONOGRAM HEART CAKES

3 Roll a small amount of chocolate rolled fondant into a thin rope long enough to cover the circumference of 8 hearts. Brush the bottom of each cake thinly with edible glue or alcohol and lay the "rope" around the sides.

4 Gently push the crimper all around the bottoms, creating a continuous, patterned border.

5 Mix a small amount of royal icing with pink food color and a bit of water to produce soft-peak consistency (see page 137) and put it into a decorating bag. Pipe the monogram on top of each cake.

FOR THE DOTTED HEART CAKES

6 Mix the white rolled fondant with a small amount of pink food color and roll it out onto a plastic board dusted with confectioners' sugar into a strip long enough to cover the bottom of 8 hearts. Roll once over that with the lined rolling pin to give it a lined pattern, then cut it into a long strip about ½ inch wide.

7 Brush a thin strip of edible glue around the bottom of each cake and lay the pink strip around it.

8 Pipe little dots of pink royal icing all over the top of the cakes; let dry.

FOR THE HEARTS ON HEART CAKES

9 On a plastic board dusted lightly with confectioners' sugar, roll out some pink rolled fondant until very thin. Using the heart cutter, cut out little heart shapes and dust them with pink luster dust.

10 Brush the back of each heart thinly with edible glue and randomly arrange the pink hearts all over the remaining 8 cakes; let dry.

Rococo Cupcakes

A lot of my designs are inspired by fashion and jewelery.
The inspiration for these cupcakes comes from a photograph I saw in a bridal
magazine of a beautiful French antique-style looped earring studded with
little lilac blossoms and draped jewels, worn by a model in a frilled eau-de-Nil
dress. The whole effect is very Marie Antoinette. I love the color
combination of green, lilac, and gold. Let them eat cake...

FOR 12 CUPCAKES

about 5 oz. gum paste

purple and green food colors

confectioners' sugar or cornstarch
    for dusting

small amount of royal icing

12 cupcakes (flavored to your choice),
    made from 1½ recipe quantities of
    Victoria sponge cake baked in gold
    cupcake cases, soaked with syrup, and iced
    with eau-de-Nil colored fondant icing, as
    described on pages 133–5

pink or silver sparkling edible pearls

TOOLS

SMALL BOWLS

SMALL PLASTIC BOARD

SMALL ROLLING PIN

PLASTIC WRAP

PETUNIA FLOWER CUTTER

FOAM PAD

BONE TOOL

FLOWER VEINER

SMALL PAINTER'S PALETTE

SMALL CALYX CUTTER

PAPER DECORATING BAGS (SEE PAGE 137)

PAIR OF SCISSORS

1 Mix the gum paste with the purple food color to produce a soft lilac shade.

2 On the plastic board lightly dusted with confectioners' sugar or cornstarch, roll some of this lilac paste out very thinly. Cover the rest with plastic wrap to prevent it drying out.

3 Using the petunia cutter, cut out 12 large flower shapes, place them on top of the foam pad, and smooth the edges using the bone tool. Press the flower veiner gently on top of each flower and place it into a well of a painter's palette to let it dry in a curved shape.

4 Roll out the remaining paste and, using a small calyx cutter, cut out about 120 small flowers. Slightly curve them between your fingers and let them dry. (You will need about 10 small flowers per cupcake.)

5 Mix a small amount of royal icing with purple food color to a soft lilac shade and put into a piping bag. Snip a small tip off the bag and pipe the drapes and loops around the sides of each cupcake. First, divide the circumference of the cupcake into 10 even sections and mark them with small dots around edge. Pipe and lift your bag from dot to dot by letting the line fall down slightly. Let the first row of swags dry.

6 Once these are completely dry, pipe the next row of swags either in between or slightly lower than the previous one. This way you will be able to create different patterns and designs.

7 Using small dabs of icing, stick one large flower in the middle of each cupcake and the little flowers evenly around the side of each. Arrange the edible pearls in the middle of each flower.

8 Mix a small amount of icing with green food color and put it into a fresh decorating bag.

9 Snip the tip off in a V shape and pipe small leaves around all the flowers. (Be careful when lifting the cupcakes, as the piping around the sides will be very fragile.)

White Spring Nosegays

This is a unique idea for little miniature wedding cakes or bridesmaids' gifts. You can use flowers to match your bridal bouquet and recreate an edible version. As these are incredibly time-consuming to make, I recommend using them for smaller weddings or events.

FOR 16 CAKES

about 9 oz. white gum paste
small amount of white vegetable shortening
confectioners' sugar or cornstarch for dusting
about 2¼ lb. white rolled fondant icing
green food color
16 miniature cakes (2-in. diameter),
    made from a 10-in. square of
    basic Victoria sponge cake mixture,
    flavored and soaked to your choice,
    covered with marzipan and a thin layer
    of white rolled fondant (see pages 122–31)
edible glue
small amount of royal icing (see page 136)

TOOLS

SMALL PLASTIC BOARD
SMALL ROLLING PIN
SMALL STEPHANOTIS CUTTER
PLASTIC WRAP
STAY-FRESH MAT
FOAM PAD
FLOWER/LEAF SHAPER TOOL
CAKE SMOOTHER
SMALL KITCHEN KNIFE
SMALL ARTIST'S BRUSH
PAPER DECORATING BAG (SEE PAGE 137)
PAIR OF SCISSORS

TO MAKE THE FLOWERS (YOU WILL NEED ABOUT 30 PER CAKE)

→1 Knead the gum paste with a little shortening until smooth and pliable.

→2 On a plastic board lightly dusted with confectioners' sugar or cornstarch, roll out a small piece of gum paste very thinly. Cut out the little flowers using the stephanotis cutter (see 1, page 63). Keep the remaining paste covered in plastic wrap to prevent it drying out.

→3 Keeping the flowers not being used covered with the stay-fresh mat, place a few at a time on the foam pad and push a line from the middle down each petal using the shaper tool (see 2, page 63). This way the petals will slightly curve inward; let dry.

→4 Pipe little dots of royal icing into the middle of each flower (see 3, page 63); let dry.

TO MAKE THE FLOWER STEMS

→5 Divide the rolled fondant into 4 equal pieces and mix 3 of them with various amounts of green food color to make 3 different shades of green; leave the rest white.

6 To make the stems, roll a small piece of each color green out to a thin strip using the cake smoother, and cut into pieces long enough to cover the sides of the cakes (see 4).

7 Brush the sides of each cake with edible glue and stick the stems around in alternating shades of green (see 5). Push them flat onto the side of the cake using a cake smoother (see 6). Trim off the excess at the top with a sharp knife (see 7).

TO FINISH THE TOP OF THE CAKES WITH FLOWERS

8 Roll a small piece of white rolled fondant to a ball, and push it down to a dome shape large enough to cover the top of a cake. Stick it on top of a cake using a dab of royal icing (see 8). Do the same for the other cakes.

9 Using little dabs of royal icing, stick one layer of flowers all over each dome (see 9). Stick a second layer of flowers in between the gaps of the first; let dry.

Tiffany-Style Sugar Boxes

No other gift box is as recognizable as the Tiffany box.
A timeless symbol of elegance and romance, and an object of desire for many,
it is often given as a wedding favor, containing a precious gift. You can,
of course, splash out and get the original; or you can make these pretty little
sugar boxes inspired by Tiffany and fill them with sugared almonds or any
gift you like. If you keep them in a dry place, they will last for months.

FOR 10 SUGAR BOXES

about 1¼ lb. white rolled gum paste

willow-green food color and baby-blue
    food color

confectioners' sugar or cornstarch for dusting

edible glue

white edible luster dust

small amount of royal icing (see page 136)

TOOLS

SMALL NONSTICK PLASTIC BOARD

PLASTIC WRAP

SMALL ROLLING PIN

SMALL KITCHEN KNIFE

2 CUBES OF POLYSTYRENE, ONE ABOUT
    2 INCHES, THE OTHER JUST SLIGHTLY LARGER

SMALL BRUSH

PAPER TOWELS

PAPER DECORATING BAG (SEE PAGE 137)

PAIR OF SCISSORS

1 Color half of the rolled gum paste with a little green and blue to make a Tiffany blue as shown. Cover this and the other piece of rolled gum paste separately with plastic wrap and let them rest for about half an hour until the rolled gum paste feels flexible and stretchy.

2 On a plastic board dusted with confectioners' sugar or cornstarch, roll out a piece of green rolled gum paste to a thickness of about ⅛ inch. Turn it over and cut out a square large enough to cover the base of the smaller polystyrene cube. Mark a square in the middle for the bottom and cut an incision down to each corner as shown on page 66.

3 Lift the gum paste off the board, dust the cube well with confectioners' sugar or cornstarch and lay the icing over its top so all 4 "walls" of the rolled gum paste are falling down the sides. Thinly brush the edges with edible glue and stick the sides together. Leave it to dry in this position for a couple of hours.

4 Once it is almost dry, carefully remove the rolled gum paste from the template so the inside can dry. Make 9 more boxes the same way.

5 Repeat the procedure using the larger polystyrene cube as a guide, but only going one-third of the way down the sides with the paste to make 10 "lids."

6 While the boxes and lids are drying, make the white sugar bows. On the plastic board dusted with confectioners' sugar or cornstarch, thinly roll out the white rolled gum paste and cut it into strips about ⅝ inch wide. You will need one strip about 3¼ inches long and one about 1¼ inches long. Brush both with white edible luster dust on one side.

7 Turn the longer strip over so the luster is facing down, fold both ends over to the middle and glue them down, supporting the loops of the bow with paper towels. Fold the shorter strip over the seam and fix it with edible glue; let dry.

8 Once the boxes and lids are dry, lay a strip of white paste down each side of the boxes for the sugar ribbons. Make sure the ribbons of the lids join with the ribbons of the boxes when putting them together.

9 Cut out the 2 short pieces for the bow endings and stick them on top of the lid. Place the bow on top; let dry.

Spring Blossom Cupcakes

Delicately handcrafted pastel-colored spring flowers give these delicious chocolate cupcakes a fresh and romantic look. They look particularly pretty arranged on a vintage-style cake stand and are ideal for a spring wedding in a beautiful country garden.

FOR 12 CUP CAKES

about 5 oz. white gum paste

small amount of white vegetable shortening

violet, dusky-pink, green, and yellow food colors

confectioners' sugar or cornstarch for dusting

small amount of royal icing (see page 136)

yellow blossom tint dusting color

12 cupcakes made using 1½ recipe quantities of rich dark chocolate sponge cake (see page 124), baked in silver baking cups (see pages 133–4), and iced with about 1 cup chocolate ganache (see page 126)

TOOLS

PLASTIC WRAP

NONSTICK BOARD WITH HOLES (CELBOARD)

SMALL ROLLING PIN

SMALL PETUNIA CUTTER

FLOWER FOAM PAD WITH HOLES (CELPAD)

BONE TOOL

VEINING TOOL

PETAL FLUTING/POINTED END TOOL

SMALL BOWLS

ICING SPATULA

PAPER DECORATING BAGS (SEE PAGE 137)

SMALL STAR PIPING TIP

SMALL PRIMROSE CUTTER

TOOTHPICK OR CELSTICK

VIOLET CUTTER

SERRATED AND TAPER CONE TOOL

STAYFRESH MULTI MAT

▶1 Knead the gum paste with a small amount of white shortening until smooth and pliable. Divide it into 3 equal parts and mix one with violet and one with dusky pink to a light pastel shade. Keep the 3 pieces of paste separate, covered in plastic wrap until later use.

FOR THE PETUNIAS

▶2 On the part of the plastic board with the largest hole, dusted with confectioners' sugar, roll a small amount of the dusky-pink paste out until very thin. Turn the paste upside down and place the petunia cutter over the top with the knob of paste in the middle.

Cut out the flower shape and transfer it onto the foam pad, placing the knob of paste inside the large hole.

▶3 Gently run the bone tool over the edges and then roll the veining tool across each petal. Gently shape the middle of the flower around the bone tool and slightly curve the petals with your fingers. Repeat to make about 12 petunias, then let dry, keeping the rest of the paste covered with plastic wrap.

▶4 Once the flowers are dry, mix a small amount of royal icing with green food color and put it in a decorating bag fitted with a star piping tip. Pipe a small star inside the well of each.

▶5 Mix a small amount of royal icing with yellow food color. Put it in a decorating bag, cut off a small tip, and pipe little yellow dots for the stamens on top of the green middles; let dry.

FOR THE PRIMROSES

6 On the part of the plastic board with the medium-size hole, lightly dusted with confectioners' sugar, roll out a small amount of the white gum paste thinly. Turn the paste upside down and place the primrose cutter over the top with the knob of paste in the middle. Cut out the flower shape and transfer it to the foam pad, placing the knob of paste inside the medium-size hole.

7 Using a toothpick or Celstick, roll over each petal to stretch it. Pick up the flower with your fingers and gently push the serrated tip of the taper cone tool into the middle of the primrose. Repeat for about 24 primroses; let dry.

8 Once the primroses are dry, dust the middle of the flowers lightly with the yellow blossom tint, using a fine brush.

9 Mix a small amount of icing with green food color, put it in a decorating bag and pipe a small dot into the middle of each primrose.

FOR THE VIOLETS

10 On the part of the plastic board with the smallest hole, lightly dusted with confectioners' sugar, roll out a small amount of the violet gum paste thinly. Turn the paste upside down and place the violet cutter over the top with the knob of paste in the middle.

11 Cut out the flower shape and transfer it onto the foam pad with the knob of paste facing up. Gently run the bone tool from the outer edge of each petal toward the middle. This will curve up the petals.

12 Pick up a violet blossom with your fingers and gently push the smooth end of the taper cone tool into the flower middle. Repeat to make about 36 violets; let dry.

TO FINISH

13 Mix a small amount of royal icing with yellow food color and pipe a small dot into the middle of each flower, covering the hole.

14 Once all the flowers are dry, arrange them on top of the cupcakes.

Large Cakes

American Sweetheart

Romantically kitsch and sugary sweet, this cake with tiny little pink rosebuds and sugar heart motifs couldn't be more appealing and girly. As such, it is perfectly suited to something like a bridal shower party.

FOR ABOUT 70 PORTIONS

3 round cake tiers, (8 in., 6 in., and 4 in. in diameter), made from 3½ quantities of basic Victoria sponge cake, flavored to choice (see pages 122–5), covered with marzipan, and then rolled fondant icing colored pastel pink for top and bottom tiers, and dark pink for the middle tier, each set on a matching thick cake board (see pages 129–31)

about 4 oz. soft-peak royal icing (see pages 136–7)

pink and green food colors

1lb. 2oz. white rolled fondant icing

confectioners' sugar for dusting

edible glue or clear alcohol

TOOLS

SMALL PLASTIC BOARD

SMALL ROLLING PIN

SMALL KITCHEN KNIFE

PAPER DECORATING BAGS (SEE PAGE 137)

SMALL ICING SPATULA

SMALL BOWL

PAIR OF SCISSORS

HEART-SHAPED COOKIE CUTTER (ABOUT 2-IN. DIAMETER)

SMALL BRUSH

8 CAKE DOWELS

SCRIBBLER

WAX PAPER

2 YD. WIDE PINK SATIN RIBBON, ½ IN. WIDE

Make and cover the 3 cakes at least 1 or 2 days ahead and trim the bases of the bottom and top tiers with ribbon, securing it in place with a little royal icing.

1 Adjust the scribbler to a measure of about 1 inch and carefully take it around the middle tier as shown (see 1, page 77), or measure approximately 1½-inches up the side of the cake, to mark the top limit of the icing border.

2 Divide the soft-peak royal icing into 3 equal portions and color it 2 shades of pink and one green, then fill each color into a decorating bag. Place the middle cake tier on top of a piece of wax paper and pipe a row of ¾-inch-long stripes in alternating colors around the bottom (see 2, page 77). Finish each strip with a dot at the bottom and the top; let dry. Keep some of the green-colored icing (covered) for later use.

3 Knead the white rolled fondant until it is soft and pliable. Divide it in 2 portions and then mix each half with a different amount of pink food color to make 2 different shades of pink.

4 On a plastic board lightly dusted with confectioners' sugar, roll out some of the pink paste to a long, thin strip, then trim the edges and cut it into small pieces of about ½ x 1½ inches. Roll each strip up into a little rosebud and let them dry (see 3–5). You will need about 250 dark-pink buds and 20 pale-pink buds.

5 Roll the remaining pale-pink paste out to a thickness of about ½ inch and cut out heart shapes from it.

6 Lightly mark the bottom tier into 8 sections radially, like a wheel, and lightly brush the back of a heart with edible glue or clear alcohol (see 6), then stick it onto the cake at the outer part of each section (see 7).

7 Stick a row of dark-pink rosebuds around the outside of each heart, using little dabs of royal icing (see 8). Arrange the pale-pink rosebuds individually over the middle tier and the remaining dark-pink buds in clusters of 3 all over the top tier.

8 Fill the remaining green icing into a decorating bag. Cut the tip off in a V shape and pipe small leaves around the rosebuds (see 9); let dry.

9 Assemble the cakes with 4 dowels each for the bottom and middle tiers, as described on page 132.

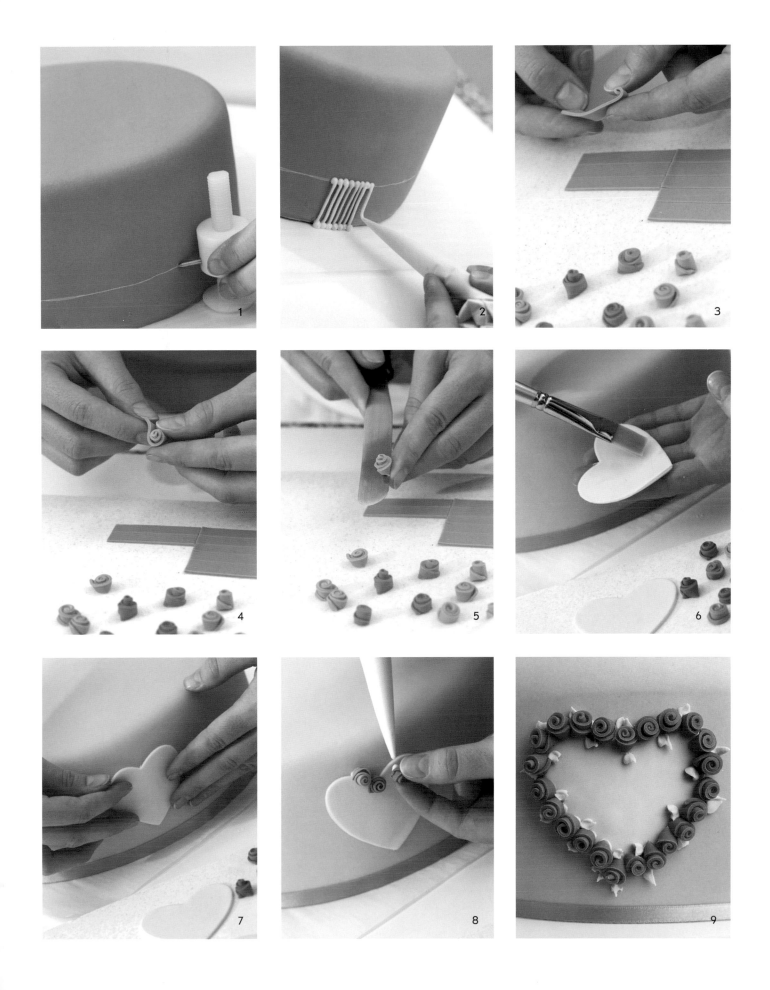

Butterfly Chocolate Cake

This clever and simple design is ideal for a not-so-traditional wedding.
Chocolate brown combined with muted pastel colors
is a very modish look right now. Some of my favorite pastels
to use in this way are dusky pink, sage green, or taupe.

FOR 120 PORTIONS

small amount of white vegetable shortening
about 10 oz. royal icing (see page 136)
dark-brown and blue food colors
3 round cake tiers (10 in., 7 in., and 4 in.),
    made from 6 quantities rich dark chocolate
    cake (see page 124), layered with ganache
    (see page 126), iced with marzipan and
    dark-brown chocolate-flavored rolled
    fondant (see pages 129–30), assembled on
    a 14-in. round cake board covered in
    dark-brown, chocolate-flavored rolled
    fondant (page 131)

TOOLS

SHEET OF CELLOPHANE
SMALL BOWLS
SMALL ICING SPATULA
PAPER DECORATING BAGS (SEE PAGE 137)
PAIR OF SCISSORS
PIECE OF THIN CARDBOARD
WAX PAPER
ABOUT 3½ YD. CHOCOLATE-BROWN
    GROSGRAIN RIBBON, ⅝ IN. WIDE
METAL PIN

Make the butterflies 2 days ahead.

→1 Rub a very thin layer of shortening over a sheet of cellophane. Lay it on top of the butterfly template (see the inside-back cover) and, using soft-peak (see page 137) chocolate-brown royal icing, pipe the outline of the wings (see 1); let dry.

→2 When dry, flood the wing middles with blue-colored runny icing (see page 137 and 2-3); let dry overnight.

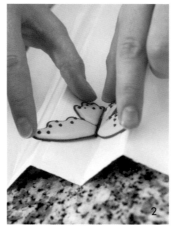

3 Once the blue icing is completely dry, decorate the wings with small dots in soft-peak chocolate-brown icing; let dry.

4 Fold a piece of cardboard to a V shape to support the wings when sticking them together and line it with a piece of wax paper.

5 Pipe a short line of soft-peak chocolate-brown icing into the fold of the paper. Lift the wings off the cellophane and stick them into the brown icing (see 1 and 2). Pipe the body down the middle of the wings over the original brown icing (see 3); leave to dry overnight.

TO DECORATE THE CAKE

6 Cut the ribbon into 4 pieces to cover the bottom of each tier and the cake board. Fix the ribbon around the board with a pin and the ribbon around the cake tiers with dabs of stiff-peak chocolate-brown icing (see page 137).

7 Using soft-peak blue royal icing, pipe small dots evenly around each side of the ribbon and around the edge of the cake board.

8 Arrange the butterflies all over the cake, fixing them in place with dabs of stiff chocolate-brown icing.

Brush-Embroidered Daisy Cake

To create a vintage-style look here, I used a technique called
"brush embroidery" for which I painted the daisy design on the cake with a
brush, using very lightly colored royal icing.

FOR 70 PORTIONS

3 round cake tiers, (8 in., 6 in., and 4 in. in
    diameter), made from 3½ recipe quantities
    of basic Victoria sponge cake, flavored to
    your choice (see pages 122–5) and covered
    with marzipan (see pages 129–30)
4½ lb. ready-made ivory rolled fondant icing
about 4 oz. white gum
small amount of white vegetable shortening
cornstarch for dusting
about 10 oz. soft-peak royal icing (see pages
    136–7)
yellow and green food colors

TOOLS

LARGE AND SMALL ROLLING PINS
2 CAKE SMOOTHERS
DAISY PATCHWORK CUTTERS
VEINED DAISY PLUNGER CUTTER
SMALL NONSTICK PLASTIC BOARD
FLOWER FOAM PAD OR CELPAD
STAYFRESH MULTI MAT
CEL STICK OR TOOTHPICK
COLOR MIXING PALETTE
SMALL BOWLS
SPATULA
PAPER DECORATING BAGS (SEE PAGE 137)
PAIR OF SCISSORS
FINE ARTIST'S BRUSHES
8 CAKE DOWELS
¼-IN. MARZIPAN SPACERS

Make and cover the cakes 1 or 2 days ahead.

EMBOSSING THE CAKE

◗1 Cover each cake with the ivory rolled fondant icing as described on pages 129–30.

◗2 While the rolled fondant is still soft, gently impress the daisy patchwork cutters into
it to create the embossing (see 1 overleaf). Leave the fondant icing to dry overnight.

MAKING THE DAISY FLOWERS

◗3 In the meanwhile, make the daisy flowers. Mix the gum paste with a small amount
of shortening and knead it until it is smooth and pliable.

4 On a plastic board dusted with cornstarch, roll out the paste until very thin. Using the daisy plunger cutter, cut out 5 daisies and place one flower at a time on the foam pad. Keep the others covered with the multi mat.

5 Roll the cel stick or toothpick over each petal to stretch it. Then carefully lay it over the well of a color mixing palette and push the middle down with a small rolling pin (see 2); let it dry. Repeat to make the remaining daisies.

6 Once dry, color some of the soft-peak royal icing yellow and pipe small dots into the flowers' middles. Reserve the rest of the yellow icing for later.

BRUSH-EMBROIDERING THE CAKE

7 Divide the remaining icing in half and color one half very pale green. Start with the green leaves. Pipe the outline using soft peak white icing for the outside and a very pale green soft-peak icing for the inside of the leaf shape. Take a fine artist's brush dampened with water and pull it from the outside to the middle of the leaf, which will create the leaf veins (see 3). Repeat with all the leaves, cleaning your brush from time to time.

8 When finished with the leaves, pipe the white outline for the daisy petals and again brush the icing from the outside edge toward the petal middle with a damp brush. Repeat for all the daisy petals, cleaning your brush from time to time. For the middles, pipe little dots of the yellow icing into the middle of each daisy.

9 Once the icing is dry, assemble the cakes with 4 dowels between each tier as described on pages 132–3.

10 With the remaining white icing, pipe small dots with a ¼-inch gap between them around the bottom of each tier.

11 Arrange the daisies on top of the cake, fixing them in place with a dab of icing.

Bed of Roses

I was commissioned to create a three-foot square version of this amazing cake for a wedding. It was a big challenge, as I had to make more than 1,500 roses to cover such a huge area. After days of making roses, I finally delivered the cake to the venue, utterly exhausted, with swollen hands and covered in glitter. But I was really proud of my achievement. The Bed of Roses made an enormous impact and everyone who saw it was stunned. Since then, it has become one of my best-selling creations and deserves a place in this book as one of the most romantic cakes I have ever designed.

FOR 40 TO 60 PORTIONS

2 lb. red rolled fondant icing

small amount of royal icing (see page 136)

about 2½ lb. marzipan

red food color

confectioners' sugar for dusting

magenta edible glitter

one 8-in. square single layer sponge cake, using 1 recipe quantity of basic Victoria sponge cake batter, flavored to your choice (see pages 122–3), covered with red marzipan (see pages 129–30)

TOOLS

12-IN. SQUARE CAKE BOARD

ABOUT 1½ YD. FUCHSIA-PINK RIBBON, ⅝ IN. WIDE

METAL PIN

SMALL ICING SPATULA

PAPER DECORATING BAG (SEE PAGE 137)

PAIR OF SCISSORS

PLASTIC WRAP

2 SHEETS OF CELLOPHANE

Prepare the cake board 2 or 3 days in advance and make your roses at least one day in ahead.

1 Cover the cake board with the red rolled fondant icing and decorate the sides with fuchsia ribbon as described on page 129–31.

2 Spread a thin layer of royal icing in the middle of the iced cake board and place the cake on top; let dry.

3 Color the marzipan deep red. Keep it covered in plastic wrap to prevent it drying out.

Make the rosebuds—and you also need a rosebud as the heart of each larger rose. (The number of roses you need to cover this cake depends on the size of your roses. For the cake illustrated, I used about 80 small rosebuds and about 20 larger open roses.)

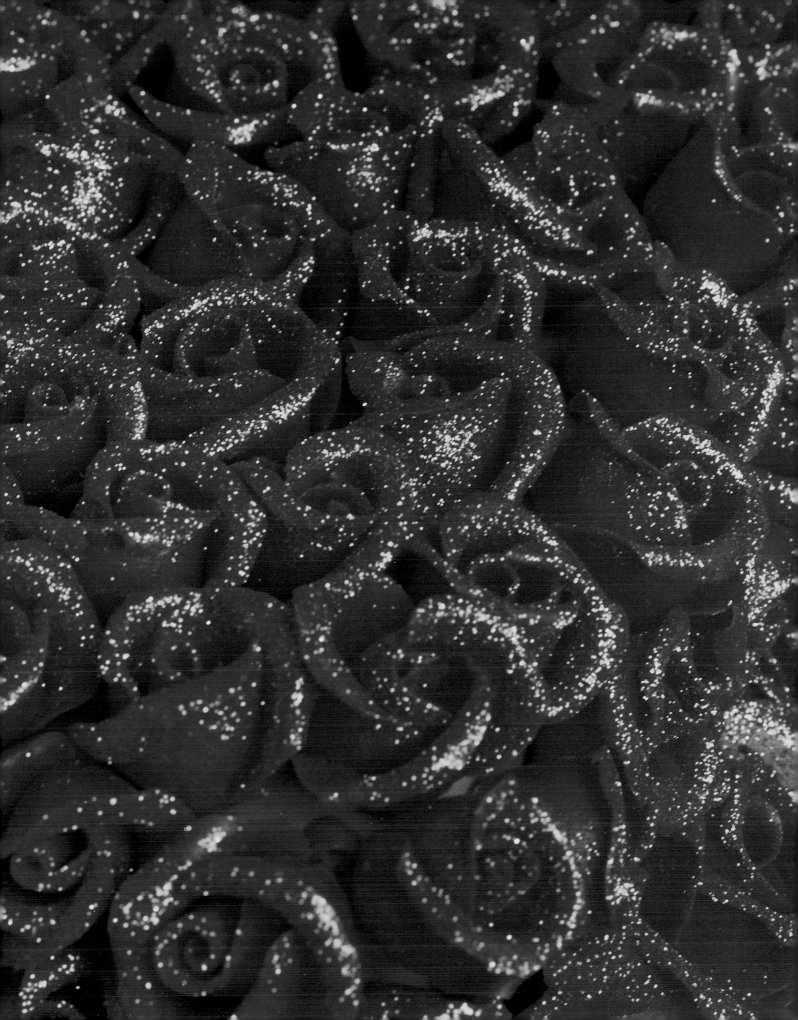

4 For each rosebud, you need 3 hazelnut-size balls of marzipan and one twice as large.

5 Place these pieces of marzipan between 2 sheets of cellophane (see 1) and start with the larger one by pushing it down sideways to make it longer, and then flatten one long side with your thumb until it is very thin (see 2). Dusting the marzipan with confectioners' sugar helps prevent it sticking.

6 For the other 2 petals, begin to push one of the smaller balls down with your thumb, starting from the middle to one side, until it forms a round petal, with one thick and one thin side. Repeat with the other balls.

7 Take the large petal first and roll it into a spiral shape, thin side up (see 3). This forms the middle of the rose.

8 Take one of the smaller petals, thin side up, and lay it around the middle over the seam (see 4).

9 Then tuck the third petal slightly inside the second petal and squeeze it around the middle (see 5).

10 Slightly curve the edge of the petals out with your fingertips (see 6).

To make the larger open roses:

11 To make each large open rose, continue by laying another 3 petals of the same size around a rosebud, each slightly overlapping the other (see 7).

12 Again, slightly curve the edge of the petals out with your fingertips to make larger roses.

13 Continue by laying another 5 petals of the same size around the rosebud, each slightly overlapping the other.

14 Slightly curve the edge of the petals out with your fingertips.

15 Pinch excess marzipan off the bottom of each rose (see 8).

To finish the decorations:

16 While still wet, dip the finished roses into the edible glitter sparkle (see 9), then leave the roses to dry overnight.

17 Once dry, stick the roses on the cake with red icing, first arranging the large roses around the sides and then putting the small buds all over the top.

My Fair Lady Cake

As the name suggests, the inspiration for this cake comes from
the famous Ascot scene designed by Cecil Beaton for the musical
My Fair Lady. Black and white is currently much in vogue for urban
weddings, so this cake design is proving very popular.

FOR 70 PORTIONS

1 lb. 2 oz. gum paste

small amount of white vegetable shortening

cornstarch for dusting

edible glue

small amount of royal icing (see page 136)

black food color

confectioners' sugar for dusting

3 round cake tiers, (8 in., 6 in., and 4 in. in
diameter), made from 3½ recipe quantities
of basic Victoria sponge cake, flavored to
your choice (see pages 122–3), iced with
marzipan and white rolled fondant
(see pages 129–30)

2¼ lb. white rolled fondant icing

TOOLS

SMALL NONSTICK PLASTIC BOARD

SMALL ROLLING PIN

PLASTIC WRAP

LARGE AND MEDIUM ROSE PETAL CUTTER

FLOWER FOAM PAD

STAYFRESH MULTI MAT

BONE TOOL AND VEINING TOOL

SMALL COLOR PALETTE

SMALL ICING SPATULA

PAPER DECORATING BAGS (SEE PAGE 137)

KITCHEN KNIFE

RULER

SMALL PASTRY BRUSH

8 CAKE DOWELS

STRONG PAIR OF SCISSORS

Make your flowers at least one day ahead. You will need about 28 flowers for this cake.

▸**1** Knead the gum paste with a small amount of
shortening until smooth and pliable.

▸**2** On the plastic board lightly dusted with
cornstarch, roll out a small amount of gum paste
until very thin, keeping the rest covered with
plastic wrap so it doesn't dry out. First, cut out a
large shape using the large rose petal cutter and
place it on the foam pad.

▸**3** Run the thick end of the bone tool along the
edges until they become thin and slightly frilly.
Then roll the veining tool across each petal.

4 Place the flower in the well of a cornstarch-dusted painter's palette. Push the middle down with the end of the rolling pin and let dry. Repeat for all 28 flowers; let dry.

5 Once these are dry, repeat steps 2 to 4, using the medium rose petal cutter and place on top of the larger dry ones. Fix the flower middles in place with edible glue; let dry.

6 Once these are dry, pipe small dots of black royal icing into the flower middles.

COVERING THE CAKES WITH STRIPES

7 Knead the rolled fondant icing until smooth and pliable. Divide in half and color one piece deep black. Cover it with plastic wrap and let it rest for about 1 hour.

8 On a clean surface dusted with confectioners' sugar, roll out one piece of white and one piece of black rolled fondant, both of the same size and about ⅛ inch thick. Trim the edges and cut each piece into strips 1½ x 4 inches.

9 Stick the strips on the side of each cake in alternating colors (see 1), using edible glue to fix them in place. Trim any excess paste off the top, using a kitchen knife (see 2) and push them flat on the sides using a cake smoother (see 3); let dry.

10 Once these are dry, assemble the cake tiers, using the dowels and the instructions on page 132, as well as the dowel template on the inside back cover, to support the tiers.

Neapolitan Monogrammed Cake

Use this very graphic and contemporary design to make your
own signature cake by incorporating the initials of the bride and groom.
Chocolate-brown and cream combine well with any pastel color,
such as blue, sage green, or caramel.

FOR ABOUT 225 PORTIONS

about 4½ lb. dark-brown, chocolate-flavored
 rolled fondant icing
confectioners' sugar for dusting
2 round cake tiers, (4 in. and 14 in. in
 diameter), made from 9 recipe quantities of
 basic Victoria sponge cake, flavored to your
 choice (see pages 122–3), covered with
 marzipan and then with rolled fondant icing
 that has been colored pastel pink
 (see pages 129–30)
one 7-inch round cake tier, made from
 1½ recipe quantities of basic Victoria
 sponge cake, flavored to your choice (see
 pages 122–3), covered with marzipan and
 then with rolled fondant icing that has been
 colored ivory (see pages 129–30)
one 10-inch round cake tier, made from
 4 recipe quantities of basic Victoria sponge
 cake, flavored to your choice (see pages
 122–3), covered with marzipan and then
 with dark brown, chocolate-flavored rolled
 fondant icing (see pages 129–30)
edible glue or alcohol
about 10 oz. royal icing (see page 136)
ivory, pink, and dark-brown food colors
about 5 oz. pastel-pink rolled fondant icing

TOOLS

18-IN. ROUND THICK CAKE BOARD
SMALL SPATULA
SMALL NONSTICK PLASTIC BOARD
SMALL ROLLING PIN
ROUND COOKIE CUTTERS (1¼ AND 2 IN.)
SMALL BOWLS
PAPER DECORATING BAGS (SEE PAGE 137)
PAIR OF SCISSORS
PLASTIC WRAP
SMALL BRUSH
TILTING TURNTABLE
14 PLASTIC CAKE DOWELS
PAIR OF STRONG SCISSORS
3 YD. CHOCOLATE-BROWN SATIN RIBBON,
 ⅓ IN. WIDE
2 YD. CHOCOLATE-BROWN SATIN RIBBON,
 ⅝ IN. WIDE
24 IN. IVORY SATIN RIBBON, ⅓ IN. WIDE
METAL PIN

Make and cover the cake tiers at least 1 or 2 days ahead.

1 Cover the cake board with about 3 pounds dark-brown chocolate-flavored rolled fondant icing and leave to dry overnight.

2 Spread a thin layer of royal icing into the middle of the iced cake board and place the largest tier on top of it.

3 On a plastic board dusted with confectioners' sugar, roll out the rest of the brown rolled fondant thinly and cut out circles using a 1¼-inch round cutter. Stick them evenly spaced around the sides of the largest tier, using edible glue or alcohol to fix them in place.

4 Using soft-peak ivory royal icing (see page 137), pipe a row of tiny dots around each circle, then pipe another row of dots between every other one of the first row.

5 For the 7-inch ivory cake, repeat the same process using pastel-pink rolled fondant, a 2-inch round cutter, and brown icing for piping the dots. Leave to dry before piping on the monograms.

6 To pipe the monograms, place the cake on top of a turntable slightly tilted away from you. Using brown soft-peak royal icing, write the monograms into the middle of the pink circles.

7 Place the 10-inch brown cake on top of the turntable. Mark the side of the cake evenly into sections about 2 inches wide with tiny dots of icing. Slightly tilt the turntable away from you. With a decorating bag filled with pink soft-peak icing, pipe a drape from one mark to another, turning the cake as required.

8 Now pipe 3 small loops above each seam and finish the design with little piped dots.

9 Repeat steps 7 and 8 for the pink top tier cake using dark-brown icing.

10 Push 6 dowels into the bottom tier and 4 dowels each into the 10-inch and 7-inch cakes, using the dowel template on the inside back cover, and assemble the cake following the instructions on page 132.

11 Arrange the ribbons around the bottom of each tier, fixing the ends with icing and around the cake board, fixing the ends with a metal pin.

White Blossom Abundance

This design is ideal for beginners, as the sides of the cake are completely covered with flowers, so any little cracks in the icing can be perfectly hidden. You do need good piping skills to make the sugar flowers, but you can make them out of gum paste instead, using a simple five-petal flower cutter to achieve a very similar look.

FOR ABOUT 200 PORTIONS

about 2¼ lb. royal icing (see page 136)
ivory food color
4 round cake tiers, (12 in., 10 in., 8 in., and 6 in. in diameter), made from 13½ recipe quantities of basic Victoria sponge cake, flavored to your choice (see pages 122–3), covered with marzipan and then with ivory rolled fondant icing (see pages 129–30)
14-in. round cake board covered with ivory rolled fondant icing (see page 131)

TOOLS

WAX PAPER
PAPER DECORATING BAGS (SEE PAGE 137)
PAIR OF SCISSORS
SELECTION OF PETAL PIPING TIPS (I USE WILTON 102, 103, AND 104)
FLOWER NAIL
SMALL ICING SPATULA
SMALL BOWL
14 PLASTIC CAKE DOWELS
PAIR OF STRONG SCISSORS OR SMALL SAW
4-IN., 6-IN., 8-IN., AND 10-IN. ROUND THICK CAKE BOARDS
2½ YD. IVORY SATIN RIBBON, ⅝ IN. WIDE
PLASTIC WRAP OR DAMP CLOTH
5 METAL PINS

Make the flowers 1 or 2 days ahead. The number of flowers you will need depends on how large you pipe them. I used about 300 flowers in 3 different sizes for this cake.

1 From a sheet of wax paper, cut small squares slightly larger than the flower you want to pipe.

2 Make a paper decorating bag and snip the tip off the empty bag to produce an opening large enough to fit a metal piping tip. Drop a Wilton 104 (or PME 58R) piping tip inside the bag, narrow end first.

3 Fill the bag with stiff-peak plain white royal icing (see pages 136–7).

4 Pipe a small dot of icing on top of the flower nail, stick one of the paper squares on top and hold the nail in one hand.

5 Hold the decorating bag in the other hand at a 45-degree angle to the nail, with the wide end touching the middle of the flower nail and the narrow end pointing out and slightly raised.

6 Squeeze out the first petal and give the nail a one-fifth turn as you move the nozzle out toward the edge of the flower nail. Use less pressure as you are moving back toward the middle and curve the nozzle slightly to give the petal a natural shape. Stop squeezing as the wide end touches the middle of the nail and lift up the tip.

7 Repeat this 4 more times to make all the petals.

8 Remove the flower with the paper from the nail and leave it to dry.

9 Color some icing ivory and pipe small ivory dots into the middles as stamens.

10 Leave the flowers to dry in a warm place overnight.

TO DECORATE THE CAKE

11 Once all the flowers are dry, stick them around the side of each tier with dabs of royal icing. Mix the different sizes and use the smallest flowers to fill the gaps; let dry.

12 Push 6 dowels into the largest cake and 4 dowels each into the 10-inch and 8-inch cake, using the dowel template on the inside back cover and the instructions on page 132.

13 Cut the ribbon into 5 pieces long enough to cover the base board and the separator boards. Arrange them around each board and fix the ends with metal pins.

14 Stack the cakes on top of each other with a separator board in between each tier, starting with the largest cake board and cake at the bottom. Spread a small amount of royal icing between each tier and board to stabilize the construction.

Homage to Cath Kidston

I am a big fan of Cath Kidston's work and this wedding cake was inspired by some of her fabric and wallpaper designs. The mix of different patterns and cake shapes works particularly well, as I have tied them together by repeating colors and textures on every other tier. I have topped the cake with a crown of large handcrafted roses in luscious red with cerise-pink middles, which you can make well in advance.

FOR 320 PORTIONS

about 3 lb. ready-made pastel-pink rolled fondant icing

about 9 oz. gum paste

red, pink, and green food colors

ruby blossom tint dusting color

small amount of white vegetable shortening

about 2¼ lb. royal icing (see page 136)

2 cake tiers, (14 in. and 10 in.) square, made from 12½ recipe quantities of basic Victoria sponge cake, flavored to your choice (see pages 122–3), both covered with marzipan and then ivory and pastel-pink rolled fondant icing respectively (see pages 129–30)

2 round cake tiers, (7 in. and 4 in.), made from 2 recipe quantities of basic Victoria sponge cake, flavored to your choice (see pages 122–3), both covered with marzipan and then ivory and pastel-pink rolled fondant icing respectively (see pages 129–30)

edible glue

cornstarch for dusting

TOOLS

TWO 18-IN. SQUARE THICK CAKE BOARDS STUCK TOGETHER WITH ROYAL ICING

CAKE SMOOTHER

SELECTION OF FINE ARTIST'S BRUSHES

ROLLING PIN

ROSE PETAL CUTTER SET

ROSE LEAF CUTTERS

ROSE LEAF VEINING MAT

CALYX CUTTERS, LARGE AND SMALL

SMALL NONSTICK PLASTIC BOARD

STAYFRESH MULTI MAT

FLOWER FOAM PAD

SMALL ROLLING PIN

BONE TOOL

SHEETS OF CELLOPHANE

PAPER DECORATING BAGS (SEE PAGE 137)

3 YD. IVORY SATIN RIBBON, ⅝ IN. WIDE, FOR THE 14-IN., 7-IN., AND 4-IN. CAKE TIERS

TILTING TURNTABLE

2¼ YD. PINK MICRODOT RIBBON, 1 IN. WIDE, FOR THE 18-IN. SQUARE CAKE BOARD

METAL PIN

19 CAKE DOWELS

Cover the double cake board and make the roses about 2 days ahead.

1 Cover the double cake board with pastel-pink rolled fondant icing as described on page 131; let dry.

2 Using cerise-pink gum paste for the rose middles and deep red for the outer petals, make about 6 large open roses, 5 small rosebuds, and a couple of green leaves as described on pages 139–41. Dust and steam the finished roses with ruby blossom tint as described on page 141.

Make the rose runouts the day before.

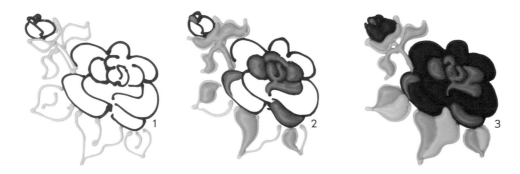

3 Place a sheet of cellophane, very thinly greased with shortening, on top of the template on the inside-back cover. Using a paper decorating bag of red soft-peak royal icing, trace the outlines of the petals, then do the same with the leaves using green icing (see 1). Repeat piping the outlines of the template 4 times, one for each side; let dry.

4 Once the outlines have dried, flood the middles of the roses with runny pink and red icing, and the leaves with 2 shades of green icing (see 2 and 3); leave to dry overnight.

DECORATE THE PINK CAKE TIERS

5 Arrange ribbon around the bottom of the 4-inch top tier, held in place with a dab of icing, and pipe small ivory dots all over it; let dry.

6 Place the 10-inch tier on top of the turntable, slightly tilted away from you. Using ivory soft-peak icing, pipe thin lines evenly from the top edge down to the bottom of the cake. You can use a smaller square cake board to act as a guide as shown; let dry.

TO ASSEMBLE AND FINISH

▶7 Arrange the pink microdot ribbon around the side of the 18-inch double cake board and fix the ends with a metal pin at the back.

▶8 Spread a thin layer of icing into the middle of the base board and carefully put the 14-inch bottom tier in place. Cut a piece of ivory satin ribbon long enough to cover the sides of the cake and lay it around the bottom. Fix the ends with a small dab of icing. Arrange the rose runouts for the bottom tier all around the sides, fixing them in place with icing.

▶9 Arrange another piece of ivory satin ribbon around the bottom of the 7-inch ivory cake and stick on the little rose runouts with icing.

▶10 To assemble the cake, use 9 dowels for the bottom tier and 5 each for the second and third, as described on page 132 and using the dowel template on the inside-back cover.

▶11 Once the cake tiers have been stacked on top of one another, arrange the roses and leaves on the top tier, using stiff royal icing to fix them in place.

Something Borrowed, Something Blue...

We normally think of accessories when it comes to this famous tradition. But why not reflect something borrowed and something blue on the cake by using some old family jewelry and blue satin bows?

FOR 250 PORTIONS

small amount of royal icing (see page 136)
ivory food color
4 round cake tiers, (14 in., 11 in., 8 in. and
    5 in. in diameter), made from 16 quantities
    of basic Victoria sponge cake, flavored to
    your choice (see pages 122–3), iced with
    marzipan and ivory rolled fondant icing (see
    pages 129–30), assembled (see page 132)
    on an 18-in. double round cake board
    covered with ivory rolled fondant icing (see
    page 131) and 24 in. ivory satin ribbon
confectioners' sugar for dusting
about 4 oz. white rolled fondant icing
white pearl luster dust
edible glue or clear alcohol

TOOLS

12 PLASTIC DOWELS
SMALL BOWLS
SMALL ICING SPATULA
PAPER DECORATING BAG (SEE PAGE 137)
ABOUT 3 1/2 YD. BLUE SATIN RIBBON, 2 3/4 IN. WIDE
2 PIECES OF JEWELRY, SUCH AS BROOCHES,
    IDEALLY HEIRLOOMS
PAIR OF SCISSORS
SMALL NONSTICK PLASTIC BOARD
SMALL ROLLING PIN
TEXTURED ROLLING PIN-SCROLL PATTERN
STEPHANOTIS CUTTER
FINE ARTIST'S BRUSH

Make and cover your cakes at least 1 or 2 days ahead.

1 Once the tiers are assembled, using ivory soft-peak (see page 137) royal icing, pipe a dotted border around the bottom of the bottom and the third tier. Tie a blue ribbon bow around the second and the fourth tiers and attach a piece of jewelry onto the middle of each bow. Trim the ribbon ends with scissors.

2 On a plastic board dusted with confectioners' sugar, thinly roll out the rolled fondant icing. Use the textured rolling pin to push a scroll design into the paste. Cut out about 20 stephanotis flower shapes and dust with white pearl luster dust. Carefully turn them upside down and brush the backs thinly with edible glue or alcohol. Arrange in clusters cascading down the cake. Repeat until you have enough flowers to cover the cake (about 120).

3 Pipe small dots of ivory-colored royal icing into the middle of the flowers.

Romantic Rose Cake

Luscious pinks and purples are one of my favorite color combinations—perfect for fall weddings. The beauty of this cake is that you can tie it in with the reception by matching the color of the roses to the ones in your bouquet.

FOR 100 PORTIONS

about 10 oz. gum paste

small amount of white vegetable shortening

pink, purple, and green food colors

plum blossom tint dusting color

edible glue

about 7 oz. rolled fondant icing

about 1 teaspoon gum tragacanth

3 round cake tiers, (10 in., 7 in., and 4 in. in diameter), made from 6 recipe quantities of basic Victoria sponge cake, flavored to your choice (see pages 122–3), iced with marzipan and white rolled fondant icing (see pages 129–30), assembled on a 14-in. round cake board covered with white rolled fondant icing (see page 131)

confectioners' sugar for dusting

small amount of royal icing (see page 136)

TOOLS

8 CAKE DOWELS

PLASTIC WRAP

3³/₄ YD. LILAC GROSGRAIN RIBBON, 1 IN. WIDE

ROSE PETAL CUTTER SET

TOOTHPICKS

FINE ARTIST'S BRUSH

CAKE SMOOTHER

SMALL NONSTICK PLASTIC BOARD

SMALL ROLLING PIN

ROSE LEAF CUTTERS

ROSE LEAF VEINING MAT

PAPER DECORATING BAG (SEE PAGE 137)

PAIR OF SCISSORS

Make your roses at least 2 days ahead.

➤1 Knead the gum paste with a small amount of white vegetable shortening until smooth and pliable, then divide it into 3 equal pieces. Color one piece of paste deep cerise pink, one lilac (a lighter purple), and one deep purple. Keep them covered with plastic wrap for later use.

➤2 For this cake I made one large open rose, 3 open roses, and 3 rosebuds (see pages 90–91), plus some extra rose petals. Dust the petals with the plum dusting color and steam (see page 141). Finish them off with the calyxes, gluing them in place; let dry.

3 Knead the rolled fondant until smooth and pliable. Add some green food color and the gum tragacanth, and mix until the paste feels slightly stretchy. Cover with plastic wrap and leave to rest for about 1 hour.

4 In the meanwhile, arrange the ribbon around the bottom of each tier of the cake as shown and secure with dots of royal icing.

5 To make the stems, roll little thin ropes out of the green rolled fondant, using the cake smoother. Cut them into different lengths and stick them on the sides of the cake with the edible glue.

TO MAKE THE ROSE LEAVES AND FINISH THE CAKE

6 On a plastic board lightly dusted with confectioners' sugar, roll the remaining green icing out until very thin. Cut out different sizes of rose leaves, push them between the veiner and attach them to the stems with edible glue or royal icing.

7 Now fix the rose heads and buds at the top of the endings of the stems with a dab of royal icing. If necessary, support them with your finger until the icing sets and use toothpicks to hold them in place. Arrange some petals down the sides of the cake.

Basics

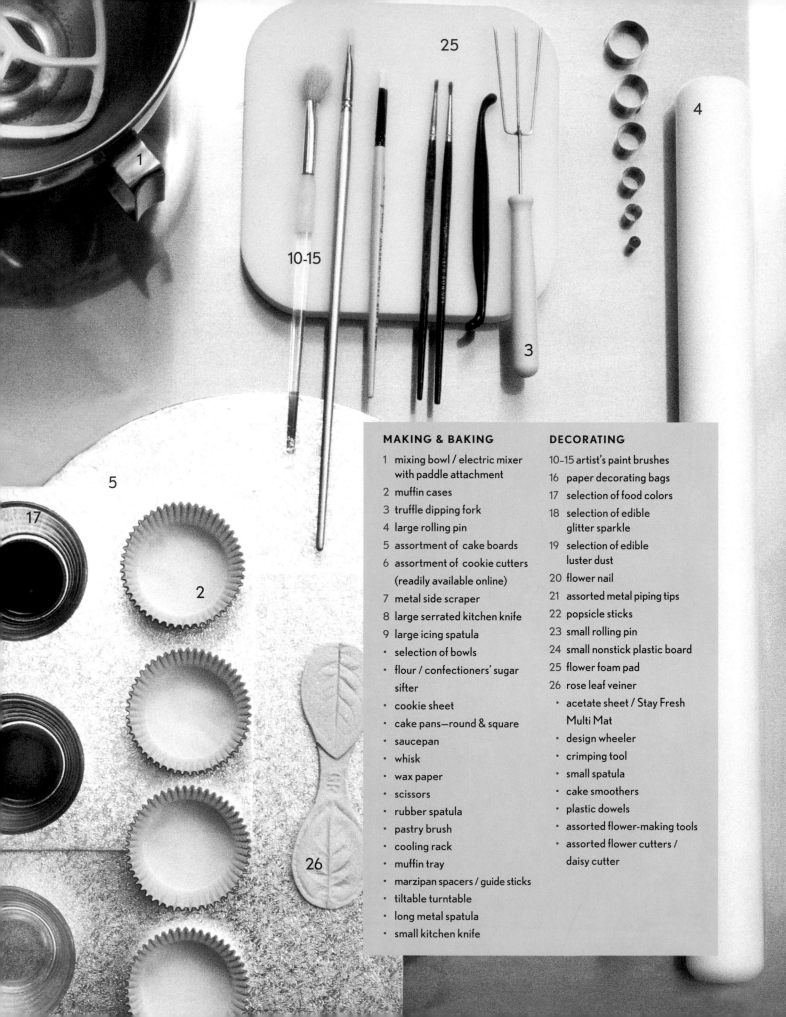

MAKING & BAKING

1 mixing bowl / electric mixer with paddle attachment
2 muffin cases
3 truffle dipping fork
4 large rolling pin
5 assortment of cake boards
6 assortment of cookie cutters (readily available online)
7 metal side scraper
8 large serrated kitchen knife
9 large icing spatula
· selection of bowls
· flour / confectioners' sugar sifter
· cookie sheet
· cake pans—round & square
· saucepan
· whisk
· wax paper
· scissors
· rubber spatula
· pastry brush
· cooling rack
· muffin tray
· marzipan spacers / guide sticks
· tiltable turntable
· long metal spatula
· small kitchen knife

DECORATING

10-15 artist's paint brushes
16 paper decorating bags
17 selection of food colors
18 selection of edible glitter sparkle
19 selection of edible luster dust
20 flower nail
21 assorted metal piping tips
22 popsicle sticks
23 small rolling pin
24 small nonstick plastic board
25 flower foam pad
26 rose leaf veiner
· acetate sheet / Stay Fresh Multi Mat
· design wheeler
· crimping tool
· small spatula
· cake smoothers
· plastic dowels
· assorted flower-making tools
· assorted flower cutters / daisy cutter

Basic Tools

Here, I set out what I think is the basic kit you'll need to make and decorate the cakes in this book. I'm definitely not saying that you'll need to get everything on my list. You can often improvize with very basic tools you already have in your kitchen. You also might prefer just to start with a few basics, such as a spatula, some wax paper to make decorating bags, a few basic tips and a rolling pin, and then slowly build up your *batterie de cuisine*, getting a few things now and then, as and when you tackle those cakes that really need more sophisticated equipment.

Baking Basic Cookies

The recipes for cookies and cakes that I have developed during the past couple of years produce results that not only taste delicious, but also have a very good texture, and—although light—are solid enough to provide an ideal base for decoration. It is important you follow each recipe carefully, as baking requires time and patience. As vital as it is to master the techniques, it is equally important to use only the best ingredients available, such as organic butter and eggs, real vanilla extract, and high-quality preserves and liqueurs.

Basic Sugar Cookies

MAKES ABOUT 25 MEDIUM-SIZE OR 12 LARGE COOKIES

Baking temperature: 350°F; baking time: 6 to 10 minutes, depending on size

1¾ sticks unsalted soft butter

1 cup sugar

1 large egg, lightly beaten

3 cups all-purpose flour, plus more for dusting

OPTIONAL FLAVORS

- For vanilla cookies, add seeds from 1 vanilla bean
- For lemon cookies, add finely grated zest of 1 lemon
- For orange cookies, add finely grated zest of 1 orange
- For chocolate cookies, replace ⅓ cup of the flour with ⅔ cup unsweetened cocoa powder

TOOLS

ELECTRIC MIXER WITH PADDLE ATTACHMENT

PLASTIC WRAP

¼-IN. MARZIPAN SPACERS

LARGE ROLLING PIN

COOKIE CUTTERS IN VARIOUS SHAPES

(SEE PAGE 142 FOR SUPPLIERS)

SMALL ICING SPATULA

COOKIE SHEET AND WAX PAPER

WIRE COOLING RACK

❧ **1** In the electric mixer with paddle attachment, cream the butter, sugar, and any flavoring until well mixed and just becoming creamy in texture. Don't overwork, or the cookies will spread during baking.

2 Beat in the egg until well combined. Sift in the flour and mix on low speed until a dough forms (see 1). Gather it into a ball, wrap it in plastic wrap, and chill it for at least 1 hour.

3 Place the dough on a floured surface and knead it briefly. Using two ¼-inch-marzipan spacers, roll it out to an even thickness (see 2).

4 Use cookie cutters to cut out the desired shapes (see 3) and, using a spatula, lay these on a cookie sheet lined with wax paper.

Chill again for about 30 minutes and heat the oven to 350°F.

5 Bake for 6 to 10 minutes, depending on size, until golden brown at the edges. Leave to cool on a wire rack. Wrapped in foil or plastic wrap, these cookies will keep well in a cool, dry place for up to a month.

Tip: Always bake equal-size cookies together to make sure they bake in the same time. If you mix different sizes, the smaller ones will be baked when the larger ones are still raw in the middle.

Gingerbread Cookies

MAKES ABOUT 40 MEDIUM-SIZE COOKIES OR 20 LARGE ONES

Baking temperature: 400°F; baking time: 8 to 12 minutes, depending on size

2¼ sticks cold salted butter, diced

1 teaspoon baking soda

4 cups all-purpose flour

for the hot mix

5 tablespoons water

1 cup packed dark brown sugar

3 tablespoons dark molasses

3 tablespoons golden syrup or light corn syrup

3 tablespoons ground ginger

3 tablespoons ground cinnamon

1 teaspoon ground cloves

TOOLS

DEEP HEAVY SAUCEPAN

WOODEN SPOON OR PLASTIC SPATULA

ELECTRIC MIXER WITH PADDLE ATTACHMENT

SIFTER

PLASTIC WRAP

¼-IN. MARZIPAN SPACERS

ROLLING PIN

ASSORTED COOKIE CUTTERS

(SEE PAGE 142 FOR SUPPLIERS)

SMALL SPATULA

COOKIE SHEET AND WAX PAPER

WIRE COOLING RACK

1 Place all the ingredients for the hot mix in a deep, heavy saucepan and bring to a boil, stirring (see 1, overleaf).

2 Once boiled, remove the pan from the heat and, using a wooden spoon or plastic spatula, carefully stir in the diced butter (see 2, overleaf).

Gingerbread Cookies *(continued)*

>3 Once well combined, add the baking soda and whisk the mix through briefly.

>4 Pour into the bowl of the electric mixer and leave to cool until just slightly warm.

>5 Once the mixture is cool, sift the flour over the top and start combining the two on low speed, using the paddle attachment, until a dough forms (see 3).

>6 Wrap the dough in plastic wrap and chill for a couple of hours or overnight.

>7 Place the chilled dough on a floured clean surface and knead it through briefly.

>8 Place the kneaded dough between two ¼-inch marzipan spacers and roll it out to an even thickness.

>9 Use the cookie cutters to cut out the desired shapes and lay them on a cookie sheet lined with waxed paper.

>10 Chill again for about 30 minutes. Heat the oven to 400°F.

>11 Bake the cookies in the heated oven for 8 to 12 minutes, depending on the cookie size, until just firm to the touch.

>12 Lift cookies off the sheet and leave to cool on a wire rack. Wrapped in foil or plastic wrap, these will keep well in a cool dry place for up to a month.

Tips
• Cookie dough or uncooked cookies can be wrapped in plastic wrap and frozen for up to 3 months.
• Cookies baked from frozen hold their shape better during baking as they don't tend to spread as much as chilled ones.
• Baked sugar cookies will keep for up to 1 month and gingerbread cookies up to 3 months in an airtight container or cookie jar.

Baking Basic Cakes

Lining a Round Cake Pan

TOOLS

CAKE PAN OF THE REQUIRED SIZE

WAX PAPER

PENCIL

PAIR OF SCISSORS

PASTRY BRUSH

VEGETABLE OIL

1 Place the cake pan on top of the wax paper, draw a line around the bottom with a pencil and use that as a guide to cut out the piece to line the bottom of the pan.

2 Then cut out a strip that is about 2 inches higher than the side of your pan and long enough to line the inside edge. Fold 1 inch of this strip over along its length and cut little snips along the folded edge up to the crease.

3. Brush the inside of the cake pan thinly with vegetable oil.

4 Place the long paper strip with the snipped edge at the bottom inside the pan to cover the side. Brush the paper snips with a little oil.

5 Now place the paper bottom on top and make sure the snips and the bottom form a sharp corner and won't allow any batter to leak through the paper lining.

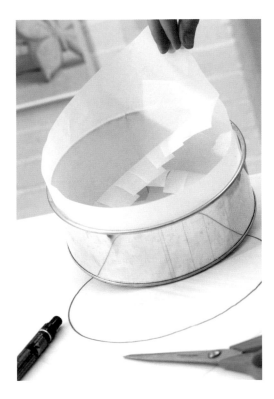

For square pans, use the same technique as above, but fold the long strip that covers the sides at the 4 corners to fit neatly inside the pan (see page 123).

Tip: As the batter naturally shrink during baking and the sides are drier than the middle of a cake, my advice is always to use a cake pan 1 inch larger than required and then trim the edges of the baked cake to the exact size you need.

Basic Victoria Sponge Cake

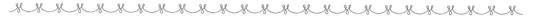

MAKES ONE 8-INCH CAKE (1/2 A TIER), 25 FONDANT FANCIES, OR 20 TO 24 CUPCAKES

(For other sizes and quantities, please refer to the guide on page 143.)

Baking temperature: 350°F; baking time: 12 to 15 minutes for cupcakes, 25 to 45 minutes for large cakes, depending on size

1¾ sticks salted butter, softened

1 cup sugar

4 large eggs

1⅓ cups self-rising flour

½ cup sugar syrup (see page 125), flavored
   to your choice

TOOLS

ELECTRIC MIXER WITH PADDLE ATTACHMENT

MIXING BOWL

CAKE PAN FOR LARGE CAKE; COOKIE SHEET FOR
   FONDANT FANCIES; MUFFIN TRAYS AND PAPER
   CUPCAKE LINERS FOR CUPCAKES

WOODEN SKEWER

WAX PAPER

LARGE SPATULA

SMALL SPOON OR LARGE PLASTIC DECORATING
   BAG

WIRE COOLING RACK

Optional Flavors

• For vanilla cake, add the seeds of 1 vanilla bean

• For lemon cake, add the finely grated zest
  of 2 lemons

• For orange cake, add the finely grated
  zest of 2 oranges

Tip: I recommend baking cupcakes on the same day as they will be iced, as they tend to dry out faster than large cakes.

▶1 Heat the oven to 350°F.

▶2 Place the butter, the sugar, and any flavoring in the bowl of an electric mixer and, using the paddle attachment, cream together until pale and fluffy.

▶3 Beat the eggs lightly in another bowl and slowly add to the mix, while paddling on medium speed. If the mixture starts curdling, add a little flour.

▶4 Once the eggs and butter mixture are combined, sift in the flour at low speed.

▶5 Line the required baking pan as shown opposite or on page 121. For cupcakes, place the paper cupcake liners into the muffin trays.

▶6 Spread the batter evenly into the pan using a spatula (see overleaf).

Tip: As sponge cake always rises more in the middle, spread it slightly higher around the side. For cupcakes, fill the paper cases about two-thirds full, using a small spoon or a plastic decorating bag.

▶7 Bake for 12 to 15 minutes for cupcakes and 25 to 45 minutes for large cakes, depending on size. The cake is baked when it springs back to the touch and the side is coming away from the pan. Alternatively, you can check it by inserting a clean, thin knife into the middle; it should come out clean.

▶8 While the cake is baking, make your sugar syrup.

9 Once the cake is baked, let it rest for about 15 minutes.

10 Prick the top of the cake with a wooden skewer and, using a pastry brush, soak it with the syrup while still warm. For cupcakes, wait about 10 minutes after baking before soaking the cupcakes with the sugar syrup. This way they will not absorb the syrup immediately and seem dry.

11 Once cool, remove the cake from the pan and leave to finish cooling on wire rack.

12 For large cakes, once cool, wrap them in wax paper, then foil. Store in a cool, dry place overnight.

Tips:
• I prefer to let large cakes rest overnight as they tend to crumble if cut, layered, and iced on the same day as baking.
• Sponges and cupcakes have a shelf life of up to 7 days after icing, and are suitable for freezing. If wrapped well, they can be frozen for up to 3 months.

Rich Dark Chocolate Cake

This is a little bit moister than most other chocolate cakes, but it is also denser and slightly heavier, which makes it an excellent base for tiered wedding cakes. It has a shelf life of up to 7 days after icing.

MAKES ONE 8-INCH CAKE OR 20 TO 24 CUPCAKES

Baking temperature: 325°F; baking time: about 15 minutes for cupcakes, 25 to 45 minutes for large cakes, depending on size

3 oz. semisweet couverture or other fine
    chocolate drops
3½ oz. milk
heaped packed 1 cup dark brown sugar
¾ stick salted butter, softened
2 large eggs, slightly beaten
2 cups all-purpose flour
1½ tablespoons unsweetened cocoa powder
½ teaspoon baking powder
½ teaspoon baking soda

TOOLS

CAKE PANS FOR LARGE CAKES OR FONDANT
    FANCIES; MUFFIN TRAYS AND CASES
    FOR CUPCAKES
WAX PAPER
DEEP SAUCEPAN
ELECTRIC MIXER WITH PADDLE ATTACHMENT
SIFTER
MIXING BOWL
MEASURING JUG
RUBBER SPATULA OR WOODEN SPOON

For other sizes and quantities, please refer to the guide on page 143.

➤ **1** Heat the oven to 325°F.

➤ **2** Line the required baking pan as described on page 121. For cupcakes place the muffin paper cases into the muffin trays.

➤ **3** Place the chocolate, milk, and half of the sugar into a deep saucepan and bring to a boil, while stirring occasionally.

➤ **4** Using an electric mixer with a paddle attachment, beat the butter and the remaining sugar until pale and fluffy.

➤ **5** Slowly add the eggs.

➤ **6** Sift the flour, cocoa powder, baking powder, and baking soda and add to the mixture while mixing at a low speed.

➤ **7** While the chocolate mix is still hot, using a measuring jug, slowly pour it into the batter while mixing at low speed.

➤ **8** Once combined, pour the batter from the bowl directly into the lined pan. For cupcakes, first transfer the batter into a measuring jug, as it is very liquid, and use to fill the paper cases about two-thirds full.

➤ **9** Bake for 15 minutes for cupcakes or 25 to 45 minutes for large cakes, depending on size. It is cooked when it springs back to the touch and the side is coming away from the pan. Or, insert a clean thin knife into the middle; it should come out clean.

➤ **10** Once the cake is baked, leave it to rest for about 15 minutes. Once cool, remove from the pan.

➤ **11** For storage, wrap in wax paper, then in foil and store in a cool, dry place overnight. This cake is suitable for freezing. Wrapped well, it can be frozen for up to 3 months.

Cake Fillings

Sugar Syrups

MAKES ½ CUP SUGAR SYRUP–roughly the amount needed for an 8-inch layered cake tier, a 12-inch single-tier square cake to make 25 fondant fancies, or 20 to 24 cupcakes

For vanilla syrup

5 tablespoons water

⅓ cup sugar

seeds from ½ vanilla bean or 1 teaspoon Madagascan vanilla extract

For lemon syrup

5 tablespoons freshly squeezed lemon juice

⅓ cup sugar

1 tablespoon Limoncello liqueur

For orange syrup

5 tablespoons freshly squeezed orange juice

⅓ cup sugar

1 tablespoon Grand Marnier liqueur

EQUIPMENT

DEEP SAUCEPAN

SPATULA

1 Place the water or juice and sugar in a deep saucepan and bring to a boil. Remove from the heat and leave to cool.

2 Once cool, stir in the flavorings.

3 Ideally, let the syrup infuse overnight as this will bring out the most in the flavors.

4 To store sugar syrup, keep it in an airtight bottle or container inside the refrigerator and it will last for up to 1 month.

Buttercream Frosting

Following a traditional English recipe, I use equal quantities of butter and confectioners' sugar to make my buttercream. The method is very simple and, as it is an egg-free recipe, it has a longer shelf life than most other buttercreams.

MAKES 2½ CUPS—roughly the amount you will need to layer an 8-inch cake tier or 25 small cakes

2½ sticks unsalted butter, softened

1½ cups confectioners' sugar, sifted

pinch of salt

For other quantities, please refer to the guide on page 143.

Optional Flavors

• For vanilla buttercream, add the seeds of 1 vanilla bean

• For lemon buttercream, add the finely grated zest of 2 lemons

• For orange buttercream, add the finely grated zest of 2 oranges

TOOL

ELECTRIC MIXER WITH PADDLE ATTACHMENT

◆1 Place the butter, confectioners' sugar, salt, and your choice of flavoring into the bowl of an electric mixer and, using the paddle attachment, bring the mixture together on low speed. Turn the speed up and beat the buttercream until light and fluffy.

◆2 If not using it immediately, store in a sealed container in the refrigerator and bring it back to room temperature before use. Buttercream has a shelf life of up to 2 weeks, if refrigerated.

Belgian Chocolate Ganache

MAKES 2½ CUPS—roughly the amount you will need to layer an 8-inch cake tier.

10 oz. semisweet couverture or other fine chocolate drops (minimum 53% cocoa content)

1¼ cups light cream

For other sizes and quantities, please refer to the guide on page 143.

TOOLS

HEATPROOF MIXING BOWL

SAUCEPAN

WHISK

◆1 Place the chocolate in a bowl and melt in a microwave cooker or over a bain-marie.

◆2 Place the cream in a saucepan, stir well, and heat to a bare simmer.

◆3 Pour the hot cream over the chocolate (see 1) and whisk together (see 2). Don't overwhisk the ganache, as it splits easily.

◆4 Cool slightly until just hardening (see 3) before use. It can be stored in a sealed container in the refrigerator for up to a month.

Layering and Icing Cakes

Tiered wedding cakes, and also miniature cakes, provide the option of mixing different flavors of cake. If you would like to make a tiered wedding cake with different flavors, you must bear in mind that the bottom tier has to carry the weight of the other tiers, so, therefore, a stronger cake base needs to be used for the bottom tiers and lighter cakes for the top. If you are following my recipes, for example, I recommend using chocolate cake for the lower tiers and the lighter Victoria sponge-based cakes for the upper tiers.

You will find a full portion guide and charts indicating amounts of basic cake batters, fillings, and covering required for various types and sizes of cakes on page 143. A template for the positioning of dowels to support cake tiers is also given on the inside-back cover.

Miniature Cakes

I usually bake and layer miniature cakes 3 days in advance, ice them on the next day, and add the decoration 1 day before the event.

MAKES 24 ROUND MINIATURE CAKES

12-in. square Victoria sponge cake
   (see page 122)

For the filling:

about 3 tablespoons jam, marmalade, lemon
   curd, or chocolate ganache (see page 126)

small amount of confectioners' sugar for
   dusting

about 2 cups buttercream or ganache
   (see pages 125–6), flavored to your choice

2¼ lb. marzipan

2¼ lb. rolled fondant icing

small amount of clear alcohol (I use vodka as it
   has a neutral taste) or water

TOOLS

LARGE BREAD KNIFE

LARGE SPATULA

TRAY OR PLATE

PLASTIC WRAP

SMALL ICING SPATULA

SMALL PAN

LARGE ROLLING PIN

2-IN. ROUND PASTRY CUTTER OR MOUSSE RING
   2 IN. HIGH

WAX PAPER

¼ IN. MARZIPAN SPACERS

SMALL KITCHEN KNIFE

2 CAKE SMOOTHERS

25 X 2-IN. ROUND CAKE CARDS (OPTIONAL)

1 Using a bread knife, trim the top crust off your cake, then cut it horizontally into 2 even squares.

2 Using a large metal spatula, spread one of the sponge halves with a thin layer of your chosen filling and then place the other one on top of that. Sandwiched together, the cake should be just less than 2 inches high.

3 Place the cake on top of a tray or plate and wrap it thoroughly with plastic wrap.

4 Chill the wrapped filled sponge for at least a couple of hours until it feels nice and firm.

5 Once the sponge is cool and firm, cut out 25 miniature cakes using the round, 2-inch high pastry cutter and place them on a tray lined with plastic wrap or wax paper.

6 Using a small icing spatula, carefully coat the sides and top of each of the cakes with either buttercream or ganache. Place each of the coated cakes on a little round cake card, using a tiny dab of buttercream or ganache to stick them in place. Return the cakes to the refrigerator and chill them until the coating is set.

7 Once the coating is firmly set, on a smooth surface lightly dusted with confectioners' sugar, knead one-quarter of the marzipan until smooth and pliable. Shape it into a ball and then, using the rolling pin and the marzipan spacers, roll it out to an 8-in square about ¼-inch thick.

8 Take 4 cakes out of the refrigerator. Cut the marzipan square into 4 equal pieces and lay each one centered over the top of each cake. Carefully push the marzipan down the sides so it sticks to them. Trim the excess off, using a small kitchen knife.

9 Run the cake smoothers along the sides and the top of each cake until the sides are straight and the top is nice and level.

10 Once all the cakes are covered with marzipan, thinly brush the outsides with clear alcohol or water and repeat steps 6 through 9, using rolled fondant instead of marzipan. Let dry completely before decoration, preferably overnight.

My Favorite Cake and Filling Combinations

• **Vanilla sponge cake**, infused with vanilla syrup, layered with raspberry preserve and vanilla buttercream

• **Lemon sponge cake**, infused with lemon and Limoncello syrup, layered with lemon curd and lemon buttercream

• **Orange sponge cake**, infused with orange and Grand Marnier syrup, layered with luxury orange marmalade and orange buttercream

• **Rich dark chocolate cake** layered with Belgian chocolate ganache and Bailey's cream liqueur

Large Cakes

For an 8-inch round cake tier you will need two 9-inch round sponge cakes (see the quantities guide on page 143).

For a Victoria Sponge Cake:

about 2½ cups buttercream

2 tablespoons jam, marmalade, or lemon curd

For a Rich Dark Chocolate Cake:

about 2½ cups chocolate ganache

small amount of confectioners' sugar for dusting

about 1lb. 14 oz. marzipan

small amount of clear alcohol

 (I use vodka as it has a neutral taste)

about 1lb. 14 oz. rolled fondant icing

For other sizes and quantities, please refer to the guides on page 143.

TOOLS

LARGE BREAD AND SMALL KITCHEN KNIVES

8 IN. ROUND CAKE BOARD

LARGE SPATULA

METAL SIDE SCRAPER

LARGE ROLLING PIN

¼-IN. MARZIPAN SPACERS

WAX PAPER

METAL PIN OR FINE NEEDLE

2 CAKE SMOOTHERS

PASTRY BRUSH

▶**1** Using a bread knife, trim the top crust off both cakes. Using the cake board as a template, trim the sides of each cake to the exact size of the cake board.

▶**2** Stick the bottom layer with the golden crust facing down on top of the cake board with a blob of buttercream or ganache.

▶**3** Using a metal spatula, spread it generously with fillings of your choice and then place the other piece of sponge on top.

▶**4** Coat the cake with the remaining buttercream or ganache, spreading it first over the top and then down the sides (see 1). Remove excess with a metal scraper for the sides and a large spatula for the top (see 2).

▶**5** Chill for at least 2 hours. This layer should be firmly set before applying the next.

▶**6** Once it is set, spread with another layer of buttercream or ganache and continue until the sides are straight and the top is level. Chill again until set, ideally overnight.

▶**7** Dust a working surface with confectioners' sugar, place the marzipan on top, and knead until smooth and pliable. Shape into a ball and roll out to an even circle ¼ inch thick and large enough to cover the top and sides, using the rolling pin and marzipan spacers.

1

2

8 Remove the cake from the refrigerator and place on a sheet of wax paper. Spread it with a very thin coat of buttercream or ganache and place the marzipan sheet over the top, using the rolling pin to lift it from the work surface (see 1).

9 Push it down the side, making sure there are not any air pockets trapped underneath. If any appear, prick them with the metal pin and flatten them while the marzipan is still soft. Trim excess marzipan off the sides using a kitchen knife (see 2).

10 Run the cake smoother over the top and along the sides of the cake until it looks straight and smooth (see 3). Use the palms of your hands to smooth the edge; let set for 1 or 2 days at cool room temperature.

11 Once set, brush the marzipan layer with a thin coat of clear alcohol to stick on the rolled fondant. The alcohol not only destroys any bacteria that might have built up while storing the cake, but also evaporates within minutes after its application and, therefore, creates a strong and hygienic "glue" between the marzipan and the rolled fondant. If you prefer not to use alcohol, use boiled cold water instead.

12 Repeat steps 8 through 11 using rolled fondant instead of marzipan.

Tips:
• For tiered cakes, start the preparation about 5 to 6 days before the event. For example, if the wedding is on a Saturday, bake the cakes on the Monday before and layer them on the Tuesday. Cover the cakes with marzipan on Wednesday and let it set overnight, so it has time to dry. On Thursday, cover the cakes with rolled fondant icing and let it set again overnight. This gives you the whole of Friday to apply your decorations, which you can prepare a couple of weeks in advance.

• For single tiered cakes, start about 3 to 4 days before the event, as the cake can be covered with marzipan and rolled fondant icing on the same day. To make 1 cake tier you need 2 sponge cakes of the same size.

• For a well-proportioned tiered cake, each tier should ideally be about 3½ inches high, including the cake board, before applying the marzipan and icing. Make sure all tiers have the exact same height, unless a mixture of different heights is intended.

Covering a Cake Board with Rolled Fondant Icing

Ice your cake board at least 1 or 2 days ahead, to make sure the icing is well set before placing the cake on top.

confectioners' sugar for dusting
small amount of clear alcohol or cold
    boiled water
rolled fondant icing (see quantities guide on
    page 143)

TOOLS

THICK CAKE BOARD OF THE REQUIRED SIZE
PASTRY BRUSH
ROLLING PIN
CAKE SMOOTHER
TURNTABLE
SMALL KITCHEN KNIFE
⅝-INCH-WIDE SATIN RIBBON TO COVER THE SIDES
METAL PIN, IDEALLY WITH A BEAD AT THE TOP

1 Dust the cake board thinly with confectioners' sugar and brush it with a little alcohol or water (to make a glue for the rolled fondant).

2 Roll out the fondant icing to about ⅛ inch thick and large enough to cover the cake board.

3 Using the rolling pin, lift the fondant icing and lay it over the cake board (see 1).

4 Let the cake smoother glide carefully over the surface of the fondant and push out any air bubbles.

5 Place the board on top of the turntable and push the fondant down the sides with the cake smoother (see 2).

6 Trim the excess paste off with a knife (see 3) and let the rolled fondant dry for 1 to 2 days.

7 Once the fondant is dry, wind the ribbon around the edge of the board and fix the ends with a metal pin (see 4).

  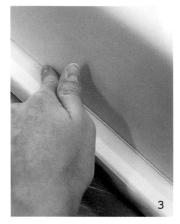

Assembling and Stacking Tiered Cakes

FOR A 3-TIER CAKE

iced cake board 3 to 4 in. larger than the bottom tier (here I used a 14-in. square board)

small amount of royal icing (see page 136)

3 iced cake tiers of different sizes, such as 10 in., 7 in., and 4 in.

TOOLS

8 PLASTIC DOWELS

SPATULA

STRONG SCISSORS OR SERRATED KNIFE

FOOD COLOR PEN

DOWEL TEMPLATE (SEE INSIDE BACK COVER)

3/4-INCH-WIDE SATIN RIBBON TO FIT THE CAKE BOTTOMS (IF REQUIRED) AND THE BOARD

METAL PIN

SMALL SPIRIT LEVEL (OPTIONAL)

PAIR OF TWEEZERS (OPTIONAL)

1 Pipe some icing in the middle of the cake board to help secure the cake.

2 Carefully lift your bottom tier with a large spatula and place it centered on top of the cake board (see 1).

3 Using the dowel template on the inside-back cover as a guide, mark the correct positions for the dowels on your cake and push 4 cake dowels vertically down into the bottom cake (see 2). Cake dowels are used to stop the upper tiers from sinking into the lower tiers.

4 Mark each dowel about ½ inch above the point where it exits the cake with a food color pen.

5 Carefully remove the dowels, line them up next to each other and saw or cut them to the same length using the average mark as a guide line. Then stick them back into the cake. To check if all the dowels have the same height, place a cake board, if at hand, on top of the dowels and check that it sits straight, ideally using a small spirit level. If you have to readjust the length of a dowel, carefully pull it out using a pair of tweezers.

6 Once happy with the length and positioning of your dowels, spread a small amount of icing into the middle of the cake, carefully lift the second tier with a spatula, and center it on top of the bottom tier.

7 Repeat steps 3 through 5 for the other tiers.

8 Measure the circumference of each tier and the cake board and cut a piece of ribbon about ½ inch longer than required in each case. Place the ribbon around the bottom of each tier and fix the ends with a small dab of icing. Use the metal pin to fix the ribbon around the cake board. Make sure all seams are at the back of the cake.

8 To cover the seams between tiers, pipe a thin line of icing along the bottom edge of each tier and, while it is still wet, run a finger over that to smooth it out (see 3).

Tip: Depending on the transport and distance to the event, it can be safer to assemble a tiered wedding cake on site. You can dowel the cakes and fix the ribbons in advance and carry the tiers individually in separate boxes.

Dipping Cupcakes and Fondant Fancies

Liquid fondant is widely used as a filling for chocolate truffles, and so on, or as a glaze for pastries. It has a very long shelf life and tastes deliciously smooth when flavored with fruit juices, extracts, or liqueurs. As it is white, it provides an ideal base for mixing brilliant colors.

Made by boiling together sugar, glucose syrup, and water, it requires experience and skill to achieve the right consistency. To keep it simple, I use ready-made fondant.

MAKES ABOUT 25

8-in. square Victoria sponge cake
    (see page 122), well soaked with syrup
    (see page 125) and layered with the filling
    of your choice (see pages 125–6)
1 heaped tablespoon strained apricot jam
confectioners' sugar for dusting
about 5 oz. marzipan
2¼ lb. ready-made Fondant
small amount of glucose

selection of liquid food colors
small amount of fruit juice, extract, or liqueur

TOOLS

SERRATED BREAD KNIFE

TRAY

PLASTIC WRAP

PASTRY BRUSH

LARGE ROLLING PIN

SMALL KNIFE

MICROWAVE OVEN

SMALL BOWLS

TRUFFLE FORK

WIRE COOLING RACK

ROUND SILVER PAPER CASES (THEY DON'T MAKE
    SQUARE ONES, BUT THESE MOLD TO SHAPE)

1 Using a bread knife, trim off the dark top layer from your cake. Turn the cake upside-down on the tray. It should have an even height of 1¼–1½ inches.

2 Wrap in plastic wrap and chill for 2 to 3 hours.

3 Once the cake is cool and firm, warm the apricot jam, unwrap the cake, and spread a thin layer of jam over the top, using the pastry brush.

4 On a work surface lightly dusted with confectioners' sugar, knead the marzipan until smooth and pliable. Shape it to a ball and roll it out to a square large enough to cover the top of the cake and about ⅛ inch thick.

5 Carefully lift it and lay it over the top of the cake (see 1). Trim the excess, if necessary.

6 Slice the marzipan-topped sponge into 1½-inch squares (see 2) and brush the tops with a thin layer of apricot jam.

7 Put the fondant in a large microwavable bowl and slowly heat it in the microwave at medium heat for about 1 minute. Stir in the glucose and heat again for about 20 seconds at a time until it is warm and runny. (Alternatively, heat it in a saucepan over very low heat, stirring. Do not let the fondant boil, or it will lose its shine.) If necessary, add a little water or sugar syrup to make it more liquid (you are looking for a thick pouring consistency).

8 If you would like to mix the fondant with different colors, divide it between plastic bowls and add a few drops of food color at a time until you achieve the desired shades. Flavor the fondant to taste.

9 Dip one cake at a time upside down into the fondant until about three-quarters of the sides are covered. To lift out, hold with one finger at the bottom and a truffle fork at the top (see 3), making sure you don't push the fork into the marzipan, or it will tear it off. Quickly shake off the excess fondant icing and place the cake onto the cooling rack, then leave for the icing to set.

10 Carefully remove the fancies from the rack by cutting them loose at the bottom using a small kitchen knife and place in the paper cases. This is best done with slightly wet fingers, to prevent the icing sticking to them. Gently push the sides of the paper case against the sides of the cake and, as they stick, they take on the square shape. Place the cakes closely next to each other until ready for decoration. Again, this helps the paper cases stay square.

11 Iced fondant fancies keep for about 7 days in a cake box or wrapped in foil. Don't store them in the refrigerator or the icing will dissolve.

Cupcakes

MAKES 20

2 heaped tablespoons strained apricot jam
20 cupcakes (see Victoria Sponge Cake,
    page 122), well soaked with sugar syrup
    (see page 125)
2¼ lb. ready-made liquid fondant
small amount of liquid glucose
small amount of fruit juice, extract, or liqueur
selection of food colors

TOOLS

PASTRY BRUSH
MICROWAVE OVEN
SMALL BOWLS
SMALL METAL SPATULA OR SPOON

➧**1** Warm the apricot jam and brush a thin
layer over the top of each cupcake to seal.

➧**2** Put the fondant in a large microwavable
bowl and slowly heat in the microwave at
medium heat for 1 minute. Stir in the
glucose and heat again for 20 seconds at a
time until warm and runny. (Or, heat in a
saucepan over very low heat, stirring. Do
not let the fondant boil, or it will lose its
shine.) If necessary, add a little water or
sugar syrup to make it more liquid (you are
looking for a thick pouring consistency).

➧**3** If you would like to mix the fondant with
different colors, divide it between plastic
bowls and add a few drops of color at a time
until you get the desired shades.

➧**4** Dip all the cupcakes of one color first into
the fondant, shake off excess, and let set
before moving on to the next color. By the
time you have dipped the last cupcakes, the

icing of the first will have set and you can
begin with the second coat of icing, as
before. Dipping each cake twice guarantees
a beautifully smooth and shiny surface.

➧**5** Any leftover fondant icing can be stored
in a bowl wrapped with plastic wrap. Before
using it again, pour some hot water over
the top to soften the hardened top layer and
leave it to soak for about 15 minutes, then
pour off the water and heat as usual.

Tip: To save fondant and washing up, I start by
mixing lighter fondant shades first and then
add more fondant and food color to the same
bowl as required. Another way of working
more economically is to mix different colored
icings to achieve a new color. For example, to
make yellow, blue, and green icings, start with
yellow in one bowl and blue in another. Then
mix these together to make the green icing.

Royal Icing and Basic Piping Techniques

Piping with royal icing is probably the one essential skill needed for most of my designs, particularly for decorating cookies. Made from confectioners' sugar and either fresh egg white or dried powdered egg white, it also makes an excellent glue for fixing sugar flowers and other decoration onto cakes. Making royal icing is a very simple procedure; if you find it daunting, however, you can buy ready-made versions from specialist cake decorating suppliers.

Royal Icing

MAKES ABOUT 2¼ LB.

about 1 oz. dried egg white powder, or whites of 4 medium eggs

8⅓ cups confectioners' sugar, sifted

squeeze of lemon juice

EQUIPMENT

SIEVE

ELECTRIC MIXER WITH PADDLE ATTACHMENT

SPOON

SEALABLE PLASTIC CONTAINER

KITCHEN CLOTH

➧ **1** If using the dried egg white, mix with ⅔ cup water and strain to get rid of any lumps. Ideally let this rest overnight in the refrigerator.

➧ **2** Place the sugar in the bowl of an electric mixer, add three-quarters of the egg-white mix or the lightly beaten egg whites and the lemon juice, and start mixing on low speed.

➧ **3** Once these are well combined, check the consistency. If the sides of the bowl still look dry and crumbly, add some more of the mixture or egg white until the icing looks almost smooth but not wet.

Stiff-peak consistency—for piping sugar flowers and leaves

Soft-peak consistency—for piping lines, dots, and borders

Runny consistency—for filling in the middles of spaces

4 Keep mixing for 4 to 5 minutes, until it reaches stiff-peak consistency.

5 Spoon into a sealable, plastic container and cover with a clean, damp cloth and the lid. Store at room temperature for up to 7 days; if using fresh egg, store in the refrigerator. The egg white can separate from the sugar after a couple of days, which will turn the icing into a dry, dense mixture. In such a case, remix at low speed until smooth and at stiff-peak consistency again. Make sure no dried icing bits sticking to the sides of your storage container get into the mixing bowl.

Royal Icing Consistencies

Throughout the book, I will refer to the three useful consistencies of royal icing (see opposite), which are important in achieving the right results. Simply thin down your basic royal icing recipe with water, a little at a time, using a spatula, until you have reached the right consistency. Always make sure you keep your icing covered with plastic wrap or a damp cloth when not using, to stop it from drying out.

Making a Paper Decorating Bag

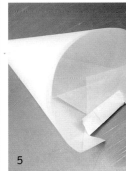

1 Take a square of wax paper, about 14 x 14 inches, and fold one corner over to the opposite one. Cut the fold with a sharp knife (see 1).

2 Take one of the resulting paper triangles and hold it with your left hand at the middle of the longest side and with your right hand at the corner on the opposite (see 2).

3 Now move your right hand over to the right corner and curl it over to the top corner, so it forms a cone (see 3).

4 Now move your left hand to the left corner and roll it around the cone until all corners meet at the top on the back of the cone.

5 Adjust the corners by moving them back and forth between your thumb and fingers until the cone forms a sharp point (see 4).

6 Fold the corners inside, tear at each side of the seam, and fold the flap inside (see 5).

7 Only half fill and close by folding the side with the seam over to the plain side twice.

Basic Piping Techniques

First snip a small tip off your decorating bag already filled with icing.

PIPING LINES

1 Hold the bag between the thumb and the fingers of your preferred hand and use the index finger of your other hand to guide the tip.

2 Touch the starting point with the tip of the bag and slowly squeeze out the icing. As you are squeezing, lift the bag slightly and pull the line straight toward you or, for example, along the sides of a cookie.

3 Once you are approaching the finishing point, gradually bring the bag down, stop squeezing and drop the line by touching the finishing point with the tip of the bag.

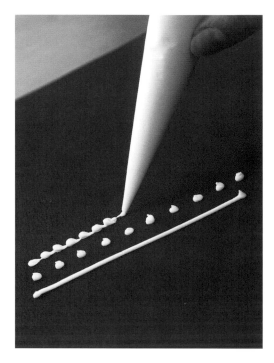

PIPING DOTS

1 Hold the tip of your decorating bag just above the surface and squeeze out the icing to produce a dot on the surface.

2 Gradually lift the tip as the dot gets larger.

3 Once the dot has reached its desired size, stop squeezing and lift off the tip.

4 If the dot forms a little peak at the top, flatten it carefully with a damp soft artist's brush.

PIPING DOTTED BORDERS

1 Start as you would for piping a dot.

2 Once the dot has reached the required size, stop squeezing and pull the tip of your bag down, stopping where the next dot should start.

3 Repeat the process, making sure the dots are all the same size and equidistant. After a while, you will notice you get into a flowing motion and your border looks nice and even.

Making Sugar Roses

Making roses from gum paste is a traditional craft that has always fascinated me. It takes time and skill making this type of rose, as each petal is shaped and stuck on individually, but I find the result very rewarding, as its fine delicate petals look almost natural, which makes it an ideal decoration for a sophisticated wedding cake. The exact amount of gum paste required does, of course, depend on the size of the roses you make.

FOR ABOUT 5 MEDIUM-SIZE OPEN ROSES

9 oz. gum paste
small amount of white vegetable shortening
selection of edible paste colors
cornstarch for dusting
edible glue
selection of blossom tint dusting colors

TOOLS

ROSE PETAL CUTTER SET
CALYX CUTTERS IN DIFFERENT SIZES
ROSE LEAF CUTTERS IN DIFFERENT SIZES
ROSE LEAF VEINING MAT
BONE TOOL
SMALL NONSTICK PLASTIC BOARD
STAY FRESH MULTI MAT
SMALL ROLLING PIN
FLOWER FOAM PAD
ABOUT 10 TEASPOONS AND 10 TABLESPOONS
WOODEN TOOTHPICKS
BLOCK OF POLYSTYRENE OR CAKE DUMMY
SELECTION OF SMALL ARTIST'S BRUSHES
SMALL SAUCEPAN
SEALABLE PLASTIC BAGS OR PLASTIC WRAP

For a rosebud you need 1 middle cone and 3 petals (page 140, see 1 to 3)

For a half-open rose you need 1 middle cone and 6 petals (page 140, see 4)

For an open rose you need 1 middle cone and 11 petals (page 140, see 5)

For a wide-open rose you need 1 middle cone and 18 petals (page 140, see 6)

The size of roses you need depends on the size of cake they will be used for.

For my Romantic Rose Cake on page 110 and Homage to Cath Kidston cake on page 104, I used cutters R1 (about 11¼ inches long) and R2 (about 8¾ inches long), but if you have a different rose cutter set it will do just as well.

Make the rose middles at least a day ahead.

1 Knead the gum paste until smooth and pliable and add a small amount of the white vegetable shortening if it feels hard and brittle.

2 Knead in the paste color as required, a little at the time. If you want to make different colors of roses, divide the paste into portions and dye them first. Wrap in a sealable plastic bag and rest for about 30 minutes. Leave some extra for the green leaves.

3 To shape the rose middles take a small piece of gum paste and shape it to a cone that is slightly shorter than the petal cutter.

4 Apply a thin layer of vegetable fat to one end of a toothpick with your fingers. Then push the greased end vertically into the

bottom of the cone. Stick the toothpick into the styrofoam or cake dummy and let the cone dry for a couple of hours, ideally overnight. Prepare all the cones you need.

TO MAKE THE ROSEBUDS

→5 To make the rose petals, place a piece of gum paste on the plastic board dusted lightly with cornstarch. Roll out until very thin, about $\frac{1}{16}$ inch. Stamp out petal shapes making sure edges are clean and sharp. Remove excess paste around the petals and wrap for later use. Cover the petals with the multi mat to stop them drying out.

→6 Place petal no. 1 onto the foam pad. Keep the remaining petals covered.

→7 Shape and stretch it by gently running the bone tool from the middle to the outside edge. Notice how the petal becomes slightly larger and the edge begins to frill.

→8 Brush the surface of the petal thinly with edible glue, using a fine artist's brush.

→9 Wrap tightly around the cone, round side up, making sure the tip is completely covered.

→10 For the second row of rose petals, take another 2 petals from the plastic board and repeat steps 8 & 9.

→11 Brush the bottom half of both petals thinly with the edible glue. Position the first of the 2 petals centered over the seam. Tuck the other slightly inside the previous petal and push the sides together. Slightly curve the edges out with your fingertips.

TO MAKE A HALF-OPEN ROSE:

→12 Continue by laying another 3 petals of the same size around the rosebud, each one slightly overlapping. Again slightly curve the edges of the petals out with your fingertips.

TO MAKE AN OPEN ROSE

➤ 13 Before continuing with the next layer of petals make sure that the half-open rose is completely dry.

➤ 14 Shape another 5 petals that are a size larger than the previous one, as described in step 7, and lay each inside a spoon dusted with cornstarch with the edges slightly overlapping the spoon. Curve the edges of the petals to the outside with your fingertips and let them dry for about 15 minutes, until they feel slightly rubbery. Letting the petals semi-dry inside a spoon gives them more volume and shape and they will look more realistic.

➤ 15 Brush the bottom half of both petals thinly with the edible glue and arrange them around the half-open rose as before. You might find the petals are now a little bit too heavy to hold up while still wet. In this case turn the rose carefully upside down on to the polystyrene block or cake dummy and leave to dry.

TO MAKE A LARGE OPEN ROSE

➤ 16 Repeat step 13 to 15 using 7 petals.

DUSTING AND STEAMING SUGAR ROSES

➤ 17 Once all roses are completely dry, you can enhance and highlight their color by dusting the edges of the petals with blossom tint colors of a complementary shade. For example, I have used plum for dusting the purple and pink roses on my Romantic Rose Cake on pages 110–113.

➤ 18 Dip a fine artist's brush into a small amount of color powder and brush the edges of the petals with it from the outside toward the middle. You have to be very careful not to spill any color as it is almost impossible to take it off. Shake off any excess powder.

➤ 19 Once you have dusted all your roses, boil some water in a small pan and hold each rose carefully over the steam for about 3 seconds. This will bring the color to life and give the rose a satinlike sheen.

TO MAKE CALYXES AND LEAVES

➤ 20 Roll out some green gum paste to about $\frac{1}{16}$ inch thick and stamp out the calyx and leave shapes. Remove the excess paste and keep it covered for later use.

➤ 21 Place the calyx onto the foam pad and gently move the bone tool over its surface from the middle toward the edges to stretch and thin the edges slightly. Keep the leaves covered until later.

➤ 22 Brush a thin layer of edible glue over the top and stick it underneath the bottom of the rose. Pinch and shape the tips with your fingers as required.

➤ 23 Place the leaves on the foam pad and again gently stretch and thin the edges with the bone tool.

➤ 24 Press each leaf in the rose leaf veiner and shape slightly with your fingers for a natural look.

Tips:
Hand-crafted sugar roses can be made weeks, or even months, in advance as they have a very long shelf life. Make sure you protect them from dust and sunlight to keep the color.

• Use a lighter color shade for the middle of the rose and a darker one for the outside petals or viceversa. This will make your rose look even more natural.

• Some blossom tints are not edible, so check the label and remove the flowers from the cake before eating if you use those colors.

Glossary

Most items are available from specialist suppliers (below), although more everyday ones can be found in supermarkets and cookware stores.

INGREDIENTS

Dried egg powder This powder is used instead of fresh egg whites in making royal icing for food safety reasons, as the dried egg white is pasteurized.

Fondant Made from sugar, water, and cream of tartar, fondant is widely used as a glaze in confectionery, as well as in pâtisserie and cake decorating. Ready-made fondant is available as a powder to be mixed with water.

Food colors The food colors used in this book are those in either liquid or paste form. The pastes are more concentrated than the liquids and, therefore, more useful for coloring rolled fondant icing and marzipans. Liquid colors mix faster and give more even results with royal icing.

Glitter, edible Make sure it is edible, not simply nontoxic.

Glucose A thick version of corn syrup used to make fondant icing to give it a beautiful shine.

Gum paste A fine and pliable paste made from confectioners' sugar, gelatin, and gum tragacanth, which dries hard, with a porcelainlike texture. It is used to make finely crafted sugar flowers.

Gum tragacanth Made from the dried sap of the Astragalus plant, this is sold as a powdered hardening agent and is mixed with rolled fondant icing to create a pliable modeling paste for making sugar flowers. It has the additional effect of making the paste set on contact with air. It can also be mixed with a little water to make an edible glue.

Luster dust, edible This non-toxic pearl dust comes in different shades. It can either be mixed to a thick paste with a drop of alcohol or applied directly with an artist's brush.

Marzipan Made from ground almonds and confectioners' sugar, marzipan is used for covering large cakes before icing, as it seals in moisture and helps to stabilize shape. It is also ideal for making flowers, as it is very easy to mold and the individual petals stick to each other naturally.

Rolled fondant A very smooth and pliable icing made from gelatin, confectioners' sugar, and water, which dries hard, but is still easy to cut. Rolled fondant is used for covering cakes and for making flowers and modeling cake decorations.

Royal icing This decorative icing made of sugar and egg white, or dried egg white, dries very hard and white, and can easily be tinted with food coloring.

EQUIPMENT

Bone (or dog bone) tool A long plastic stick with rounded ends, looking like a bone, this is used to shape rolled fondant petals.

Cake smoothers These are flat, rectangular pieces of smooth plastic, with a handle, used to smooth the marzipan and rolled fondant icing on a cake.

Cel stick This is a thin, plastic stick for shaping flowers.

Foam pad This is used as a yielding surface for thinning the edges of flowers with a bone tool (above).

Flower cutters Made of metal or plastic, flower cutters are used to cut petals and leaves out of gum paste. In this book I have used cutters to make roses, petunias, primroses and violets.

Flower nail Used for making royal icing sugar flowers. It functions as a base for the piping, as it may be turned readily in the non-piping hand.

Guide sticks Long sticks used to roll out dough or sugar paste to an even thickness.

Leaf veiner/veining mat A rubber mat used for shaping and marking leaves made of flower paste or marzipan.

Rose and leaf embosser Usually made of plastic, embossers are used to push the impression of a pattern into icing.

Rose calyx cutter Used for cutting the calyx for a rose out of flower paste or marzipan.

Side scraper Flat piece of metal (ideally stainless steel) with a straight side used for scraping excess off cake's side.

Suppliers

For general cake decorating tools and equipment:

UK

Jane Asher Party Cakes
24 Cale Street
London SW3 3QU
www.jane-asher.co.uk

Almond Art
Unit 15 & 16 Faraday Close
Gorse Lane Industrial Estate
Clacton-on-Sea, Essex
CO15 4TR
www.almondart.com

Design A Cake
30–31 Phoenix Road
Crowther Industrial Estate
Washington,
Tyne & Wear
NE38 0AD
www.design-a-cake.co.uk

Squires Shop and School
Squires House
3 Waverley Lane
Farnham, Surrey
GU9 8BB
www.squires-group.co.uk

For edible lustre and glitter sparkle:

EdAble Art
1 Stanhope Close
The Grange,
Spennymoor
Co Durham DL16 6LZ
tel 01388 816309

For Ribbons

VV Rouleaux
54 Sloane Square
London SW1W 8AX
www.vvrouleaux.com

WORLDWIDE

AUSTRALIA

CAKE DECO
Shop 7, Port Phillip Arcade
232 Flinders Street
Melbourne, Victoria
Australia
www.cakedeco.com.au

GERMANY

Tortissimo Backzubehör
Carl-Benz-Str. 6
35305 Grünberg
Deutschland
www.tortissimo.de

THE NETHERLANDS

De leukste Taarten Shop
Meeuwstraat 10
1546 LR Jisp, Holland
www.deleukstetaartenshop.nl

USA

Sugarcraft, Inc.
2715 Dixie Hwy.
Hamilton, Ohio 45015
www.sugarcraft.com

For cookie cutters

Kitchen Collectables, Inc.
8901 J. Street, Suite 2
Omaha NE 68127, USA
www.kitchengifts.com

CopperGifts.com
900 N. 32nd St
Parsons, KS 67357, USA
www.coppergifts.com

 For more information on Peggy Porschen's cookies and cakes, or to place an order, please visit her website **peggyporschen.com**

CAKE BATTER QUANTITY AND PORTION GUIDE

This chart will give an overview of what size cake you need for your number of guests and the approximate quantity of cake batter needed for the different sizes of cake pans.

The basic cake recipes in this book are based on an 8-inch cake pan, or 20 to 24 cakes, or 25 fondant fancies. Please bear in mind for each cake tier you will need 2 sponges, in other words, double the amount of cake batter, baked in 2 pans of the same size (except for the Bed of Roses Cake on page 86). The figure shown in the second column below indicates by how much the basic recipe needs to be multiplied.

I also recommend baking a cake 1 inch larger than required, it will shrink during baking and the sides are usually a bit dry. After baking, trim the edges with a serrated knife down to the exact size required, using the cake board as a guide.

Cake Pan Size (round or square)	Multiply basic recipe by	Cake Portions 1x1 inch round/square	Mini Cakes	Cup-cakes	Fondant Fancies
4 inches	¼	10 / 16			
5 inches	⅓	12 / 20			
6 inches	½	20 / 35			
7 inches	¾	25 / 45			
8 inches	1	40 / 60	9	20 to 24	25
9 inches	1⅓	50 / 80			
10 inches	2	60 / 100	16	40 to 48	36
11 inches	2½	80 / 120			
12 inches	3¼	90 / 140	25		
14 inches	4¼	130 / 185			

• If you want a large centerpiece, but only need a small amount of cake, use a fake tier in between real tiers. Tell the bride and groom, to avoid them trying to cut it.

Quantity guide for marzipan, rolled fondant icing, and buttercream or chocolate ganache fillings

The figures below give you the approximate amounts required for cakes of different sizes, round or square, with a height of 3 ½ inches.

CAKE BOARD SIZE	MARZIPAN/ ROLLED FON- DANT ICING	ROLLED FONDANT FOR CAKE BOARD	BUTTERCREAM / GANACHE
4 inches	14 oz.		⅔ cup (also 25 fondant fancies)
5 inches	1lb. 2oz.		1 cup
6 inches	1¼ lb.	10 oz.	1¼ cups
7 inches	1lb. 10oz.	14 oz.	2 cups (also 20 to 24 cupcakes)
8 inches	1¾ lb.	1¼ lb.	2½ cups (also 25 mini cakes)
9 inches	2 lb.	23 oz.	3 cups
10 inches	2¾ lb.	27 oz.	4 cups
11 inches	3 lb. 3 oz.	1¾ lb.	5⅓ cups
12 inches	3½ lb.	2 lb.	3lb. 3oz.
13 inches	4½ lb.	2lb. 2oz.	3½ lb.
14 inches	5½ lb.	2¼ lb.	4½ lb.

Acknowledgments

The success of my first book, *Pretty Party Cakes* was absolutely overwhelming. I would like to thank all the readers who have sent me the most wonderful encouraging letters and emails from all over the world, and I hope that this book will live up to your expectations and inspire you just as much.

I would also like to thank Alison Cathie, Jane O'Shea, and Helen Lewis of Quadrille Publishing for signing me up for another beautiful project and letting me explore my favorite subject area—making cakes and cookies for romantic occasions. As always, it has been an absolute joy working with all of you.

A big thank-you to my dream team: Georgia Glynn Smith for your phenomenal photography; Lewis Esson, you are my wizard of words; and Chalkley Calderwood Pratt for your beautiful eye for design and layout. Once again it has been a privilege and an inspiration to work with all of you.

None of this would have been possible without the loving support, encouragement, and inspiration of my partner Bryn; my parents Iris and Helmut; and my brother, Tom. I am eternally grateful for everything you have done for me.

Last, but not least, I would like to thank my team at Peggy Porschen Cakes and all our loyal clients for their support and trust that have made it possible for me to establish Peggy Porschen Cakes as one of the UK's leading cake design companies.

This basic butterfly template can be reduced or enlarged as required to make butterflies of the appropriate sizes.